DO
SOMETHING!

A HANDBOOK FOR
YOUNG ACTIVISTS

TO ALL THE KIDS OUT THERE ROCKING THEIR THING.

Library of Congress Cataloging-in-Publication Data is available.

ISBN 978-0-7611-5747-2

Design by Jen Browning
Additional illustrations by Phil Conigliaro
Photo Credits: Associated Press: 10 bottom. Courtesy of DoSomething.org: 10 top, 66 top, 176 top, 242 bottom, 224 top and bottom. Photography by Kate Dwek: 196 top. Getty Images: Cover, iii, viii, 42, 66 bottom, 82, 176 bottom, 186, 217, 236, 242 top. Retna Ltd. NYC: 196 bottom.

Workman books are available at special discounts when purchased in bulk for premiums and sales promotions as well as for fund-raising or educational use. Special editions or book excerpts also can be created to specification. For details, contact the Special Sales Director at the address below or send an e-mail to specialmarkets@workman.com.

Workman Publishing Company, Inc.
225 Varick Street
New York, NY 10014-4381

www.workman.com

Printed in China
First printing October 2010

10 9 8 7 6 5 4 3 2 1

NANCY LUBLIN, CEO and Chief Old Person of **DOSOMETHING.ORG**

(with Vanessa Martir and Julia Steers)

DO SOMETHING!

A HANDBOOK FOR YOUNG ACTIVISTS

WORKMAN PUBLISHING • NEW YORK

table of contents

CHAPTER 1 — see it!

What's your Thing?

PROJECT #1: The Super-Fast Find-Your-Thing Quiz   3
PROJECT #2: The Gut Test   11
PROJECT #3: Get Focused   15
PROJECT #4: Where is Your Where?   20
PROJECT #5: Rate Your Room   22
PROJECT #6: Scan Your School   26
PROJECT #7: Take a Hike   28
PROJECT #8: Read All About It   31
PROJECT #9: Get Chatty   36
SEE IT Recap   40

CHAPTER 2 — believe it!

Figure out why you care

PROJECT #10: Map the Problem   45
PROJECT #11: Fact Sheet 101   48
PROJECT #12: Ask the Experts   54
PROJECT #13: Survey Central   60
PROJECT #14: Numbers Game   64
PROJECT #15: Superhero Help   67
PROJECT #16: Fill Out Your Own Problem Map   73
11 WAYS TO BELIEVE IT   76
BELIEVE IT Recap   80

CHAPTER 3 — build it!

What are you going to do about it?

PROJECT #17: Pick a Plan   85
PROJECT #18: A Rough Draft   169
PROJECT #19: Target the Right Time   172
PROJECT #20: Location, Location, Location   177
PROJECT #21: Casting Call   180
PROJECT #22: Matchmaker   182
BUILD IT Recap   185

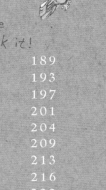

CHAPTER 4 do it!

Get out there and rock it!

PROJECT #23: On a Mission   189

PROJECT #24: Elevator Pitch   193

PROJECT #25: Debate Club   197

PROJECT #26: Make It Flow   201

PROJECT #27: Get `Em Together   204

PROJECT #28: Name It!   209

PROJECT #29: Logo Pogo   213

PROJECT #30: Spread the Word   216

PROJECT #31: Chat It Up   222

PROJECT #32: Petition Time   225

PROJECT #33: Before the Big Day   228

PROJECT #34: The Flip Side   231

DO IT Recap   234

CHAPTER 5 reflect it!

Look back on doing good

PROJECT #35: Scrapbook Star   239

PROJECT #36: In Your Shoes   243

PROJECT #37: A Final Draft   244

PROJECT #38: Numbers Game Part 2   248

PROJECT #39: Thank You Time   250

PROJECT #40: Letter to the Editor   255

PROJECT #41: Pass It On   257

REFLECT IT Recap   260

appendix

Keep track of all your notes and important information

BOOK IT   263

RESOURCES   275

CHECK OUT *DoSomething.org/book* for fun downloads, facts about important issues, starting your own Do Something Club, and other ways to get involved.

introduction

LISTEN UP! YOU DON'T HAVE TO BE a rock star or the president or even have your driver's license to change the world. You can do important things right now—like, before your head hits the pillow tonight—that can make a difference in someone's life, change something for the better, or fix an important problem.

Yeah, we know that old people tell you "You can do anything you put your mind to" and other stuff like that. **WE'RE NOT YOUR MOM.** We're not your teacher. (Ugh. There is **NO** grading in this book.) At DoSomething.org, we're helping millions of kids impact causes they care about. We know you can do something because we've seen it happen over and over again.

Young people rocking change isn't just possible; it's happening every day. Like the 12-year-old who registered over 10,000 people to donate bone marrow for people with cancer. Or the 7-year-old who taught other kids to swim. Or the 10-year-old who raised $30 by selling lemonade—and it was enough to buy dog food at a shelter for one night. **IF THEY CAN DO IT, SO CAN YOU.**

THE BOOK YOU'RE HOLDING IN YOUR HANDS IS YOUR GUIDE TO MAKING THE WORLD A BETTER PLACE. We're going to help you find your Thing—the cause you want to do something about—and then build an awesome Action Plan so you can go out there and do something! A great Action Plan can be anything from a poster campaign to raise awareness about an important issue, to a fun event to raise money for a great organization—from a petition to change something about your school, to a weekend volunteer gig. If you can't figure out what you want to do, we have tons of ideas for you with step-by-step Action Plans in Chapter 3, "Build It."

We've also given you 41 interactive projects to take you every step of the way. That may seem like a lot, but don't worry, you don't have to do all of them! Does one look boring? Skip it! Would you do one differently? Change it up! Was one really fun? Do it again!

DON'T JUST READ THIS BOOK. USE IT!

This is your journal, your notebook, your planner, your calendar. Draw in it! Paste in it! Tear it up! Fold down the corners! Make it YOURS.

Don't wait until you become the president—or that rock star! Go ahead and rock some change right now . . . turn the page. Go on. **TURN IT!**

CHAPTER I

see it!

SO, YOU WANT TO CHANGE THE WORLD? THAT'S GREAT! WHERE DO YOU START? DO YOU KNOW WHAT YOU WANT TO FIGHT FOR? IMPROVE? GET RID OF? DO THOSE DYING PENGUINS IN ANTARCTICA BUM YOU OUT? DO THE CLASSROOM LIGHTS LEFT ON ALL NIGHT MAKE YOU MAD? DOES THE THOUGHT OF PEACE IN THE MIDDLE EAST GET YOU PUMPED? IN OTHER WORDS: **WHAT'S YOUR THING? WHAT'S THE ISSUE THAT GETS YOU SAD OR MAD OR LEAVES YOU FEELING OVERWHELMED?**

MAYBE THERE'S SOME TERRIBLE PROBLEM YOU PASS ON YOUR STREET OR HEAR ABOUT IN THE NEWS, AND YOU THINK: *I NEED TO FIX THAT.* **OR MAYBE YOU JUST WANT TO MAKE A DIFFERENCE** AND DON'T KNOW WHERE TO START. YOU JUST NEED TO **SEE IT.**

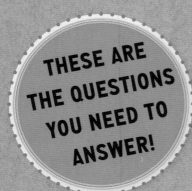

THESE ARE THE QUESTIONS YOU NEED TO ANSWER!

WHAT IS MY THING?

WHAT PART OF MY THING DO I WANT TO FOCUS ON FIRST?

WHERE IN THE WORLD DO I SEE MY THING?

WHY IS MY THING IMPORTANT?

DO PROJECTS #1 — #9 TO FIGURE IT OUT!

PROJECT #1: THE SUPER-FAST FIND-YOUR-THING QUIZ

This quick quiz will take you through 11 causes that matter—causes that could be your Thing. Unlike a math quiz, there are no right or wrong answers. The quiz will get you thinking about the problems and issues that affect your daily life: what you care about, what bothers you, what you would like to change if you could. It will help you figure out the issues that inspire you the most, the Thing that gets you pumped, the Thing you care about so much that you want to dedicate time and energy to do something about it. Don't worry; you don't have to stick with one Thing forever. You can always find something new to care about. Already know what your Thing is? Then skip this project and go straight to Project #3 on page 15.

STUFF: A pencil

TIME: 10–20 minutes. Depends how much you want to think about each answer.

STEPS

1. Fill out the cards on the following pages. Don't check YES! just because you think you *should* care. All of these issues are important but you need to figure out what is important to *you*.

2. Count the number of YES! and NOT REALLY answers and enter them in the spaces provided.

3. Look at your final counts—which Thing got the most YES! answers? If there's an obvious winner, you've got your Thing and can jump to Project #3 on page 15.

4. If more than one Thing got around the same number of YES! answers, write down the top three issues in the spaces provided and go on to Project #2 on page 11 to narrow it down to just one.

Answer these questions to find your Thing!

Is your Thing ANIMAL WELFARE?

1. Do you have a pet? If not, do you beg your folks for one every day?

   ❑ YES!   ❑ NOT REALLY

2. Are you a vegetarian because you think that people shouldn't eat animals?

   ❑ YES!   ❑ NOT REALLY

3. Are there lots of homeless or stray animals in your neighborhood? Does that make you mad?

   ❑ YES!   ❑ NOT REALLY

4. Do you live somewhere with a lot of wildlife roaming around nearby? What about farms?

   ❑ YES!   ❑ NOT REALLY

5. Do you tear up when you watch a movie about animals in trouble?

   ❑ YES!   ❑ NOT REALLY

FINAL COUNT: _____ YES!   _____ NOT REALLY

Is your Thing DISASTER RESPONSE & RELIEF?

1. Do you live in an area where there are natural disasters like tornadoes or earthquakes?

   ❑ YES!   ❑ NOT REALLY

2. Does your town have any houses that are burned out or falling apart because of a disaster?

   ❑ YES!   ❑ NOT REALLY

3. Do you know what to do if there is a fire or flood in your home?

   ❑ YES!   ❑ NOT REALLY

4. Do you know what to do if there is a disaster at your school?

   ❑ YES!   ❑ NOT REALLY

5. Do your friends know what to do in the event of a disaster?

   ❑ YES!   ❑ NOT REALLY

FINAL COUNT: _____ YES!   _____ NOT REALLY

Is your Thing DISCRIMINATION?

1. Does it make you mad when kids at school are teased because they're different?

❏ YES!   ❏ NOT REALLY

2. Do you or any of your friends feel self-conscious about your race, ethnicity, religion, or disability?

❏ YES!   ❏ NOT REALLY

3. Does your town or school have a big mix of races and ethnicities?

❏ YES!   ❏ NOT REALLY

4. Do you feel that discrimination exists in your school but people pretend it doesn't?

❏ YES!   ❏ NOT REALLY

5. Have you ever heard someone say something negative about a person's race, religion, or disability? Did it make you mad?

❏ YES!   ❏ NOT REALLY

FINAL COUNT: _____ YES!   _____ NOT REALLY

Is your Thing EDUCATION?

1. Do you love your school (most of the time)?

❏ YES!   ❏ NOT REALLY

2. Is it hard to get the teacher's attention because there are too many kids in your class?

❏ YES!   ❏ NOT REALLY

3. Do you wish that there were more music and art classes at school?

❏ YES!   ❏ NOT REALLY

4. Are your textbooks and school computers a million years old?

❏ YES!   ❏ NOT REALLY

5. Do you wish that your school had awesome after-school programs?

❏ YES!   ❏ NOT REALLY

FINAL COUNT: _____ YES!   _____ NOT REALLY

Is your Thing the ENVIRONMENT?

1. Does it drive you crazy when your friends toss their bottles and cans in the trash instead of the recycling bin?

❑ YES!   ❑ NOT REALLY

2. Does the smell of the chemicals used to clean your school make you want to gag (and fear for your brain cells)?

❑ YES!   ❑ NOT REALLY

3. Have you ever counted all the paper you throw away in a week? Would you even want to?

❑ YES!   ❑ NOT REALLY

4. Are there any bodies of water (ponds or lakes) in your town that are so polluted that you wouldn't dare dip in your toe?

❑ YES!   ❑ NOT REALLY

5. Do you wonder where the family computer went after it died? What about all those cell phones your parents have used over the years?

❑ YES!   ❑ NOT REALLY

FINAL COUNT: _____ YES!   _____ NOT REALLY

Is your Thing HEALTH & FITNESS?

1. Do you exercise every day?

❑ YES!   ❑ NOT REALLY

2. Does any of your favorite grown-ups—parents, aunts and uncles, teachers or coaches—smoke cigarettes? Do you wish they would stop?

❑ YES!   ❑ NOT REALLY

3. Does your town have pretty much only fast-food restaurants?

❑ YES!   ❑ NOT REALLY

4. Are you or anyone you love dealing with an illness like diabetes, heart disease, asthma, or cancer?

❑ YES!   ❑ NOT REALLY

5. Do you wish your school had better sports teams, longer recess, a cooler gym class, or healthier lunch options?

❑ YES!   ❑ NOT REALLY

FINAL COUNT: _____ YES!   _____ NOT REALLY

Is your Thing HUMAN RIGHTS?

1. Are you interested in what life is like for people living in foreign countries?

❑ YES! ❑ NOT REALLY

2. Do you think that all people should have the same rights?

❑ YES! ❑ NOT REALLY

3. Do you ever think about what it would be like to live in a country where you couldn't speak your mind?

❑ YES! ❑ NOT REALLY

4. Do you know any people who have immigrated to this country, or whose parents immigrated to this country, in pursuit of more freedom?

❑ YES! ❑ NOT REALLY

5. You may not love school, but do you think that every child has the right to an education?

❑ YES! ❑ NOT REALLY

FINAL COUNT: _____ YES! _____ NOT REALLY

Is your Thing HUNGER & HOMELESSNESS?

1. Are there people living on the streets of your town?

❑ YES! ❑ NOT REALLY

2. Do you know where they go for food and shelter? Do you want to?

❑ YES! ❑ NOT REALLY

3. Do you ever think about giving those old clothes you've outgrown to someone who needs them?

❑ YES! ❑ NOT REALLY

4. Are you or your friends eligible for free lunch at school?

❑ YES! ❑ NOT REALLY

5. Do you feel bad when you throw away uneaten food?

❑ YES! ❑ NOT REALLY

FINAL COUNT: _____ YES! _____ NOT REALLY

7

Is your Thing POVERTY?

1. Do you know if poverty is an issue in your town or neighborhood?

    ❑ YES!   ❑ NOT REALLY

2. Have you ever seen extreme poverty firsthand, either at home or in other parts of the world?

    ❑ YES!   ❑ NOT REALLY

3. Do you see pictures or movies or news reports about extreme poverty in the world and want to help but don't know how?

    ❑ YES!   ❑ NOT REALLY

4. Have you heard stories from your parents or grandparents about times when they didn't have enough money?

    ❑ YES!   ❑ NOT REALLY

5. Does it frustrate you that some people can have so much while others have so little?

    ❑ YES!   ❑ NOT REALLY

FINAL COUNT: _____ YES! _____ NOT REALLY

Is your Thing VIOLENCE & BULLYING?

1. Have you or your friends or siblings ever been threatened or bullied at school?

    ❑ YES!   ❑ NOT REALLY

2. Have you ever heard rumors online—about yourself or friends—that you knew weren't true?

    ❑ YES!   ❑ NOT REALLY

3. Do you have to be careful about gang violence in your town?

    ❑ YES!   ❑ NOT REALLY

4. Do you know anyone who has been the victim of violence on the street or at home?

    ❑ YES!   ❑ NOT REALLY

5. Have you ever wished you were a superhero who could go around saving people from mean people?

    ❑ YES!   ❑ NOT REALLY

FINAL COUNT: _____ YES! _____ NOT REALLY

Is your Thing **WAR & PEACE?**

1. Do you follow news about world politics and conflicts?

    ❏ YES!   ❏ NOT REALLY

2. Do you know anyone who is serving or has served in the military, or have you ever thought about joining the military?

    ❏ YES!   ❏ NOT REALLY

3. Have you ever met anyone who had to leave their homeland because of war or violence?

    ❏ YES!   ❏ NOT REALLY

4. Do you wonder what it's like to be a kid living in a war-torn country?

    ❏ YES!   ❏ NOT REALLY

5. Do you feel like you should take a stand against war?

    ❏ YES!   ❏ NOT REALLY

FINAL COUNT: _____ **YES!**   _____ **NOT REALLY**

Count them up. Is there an obvious winner? That's your Thing! If not, list the three issues that got the most YES! answers, and move on to the next project.

Write your top three issues here

THEY'RE DOING SOMETHING!

NAME: Charlie Coons, 12, California
THING: International orphans

KEEPING KIDS WARM After hearing her 16-year-old brother's firsthand account of working in orphanages in Egypt, Charlie was inspired to take action. Charlie began making fleece blankets to give some comfort to orphans around the world. In less than a year Charlie sent blankets to Egypt, Iraq, Afghanistan, Honduras, Gaza, Jordan, and most recently to Rwanda. Her project is called: Hope, Encouragement, Love, Peace (HELP). Check her out at: DoSomething.org/book.

NAME: Drew Barrymore
THING: Hunger

FEEDING THE NEED Shocked when she found out how many people go hungry around the world, Drew Barrymore donated $1 million to the World Food Programme's Against Hunger campaign. But she knew that just giving money wasn't enough! She became an ambassador for the program and travels around the world to learn more about hunger and encourage people to get involved.

PROJECT #2: THE GUT TEST

Okay, you're getting close. You've narrowed your Thing down to three possible causes, but you still don't know what to pick. Why not go with your gut? Your gut is that part of your stomach that clenches when you're nervous, flip-flops when you're excited, gets all tingly when you're mad, and aches a little when you're sad. Listening to your gut is a great way to figure out how you feel about something, because the stronger the feeling in your gut, the more passion you have for your Thing. Passion means you care, and really caring about your Thing is the first step toward believing you can do something about it.

Your reasons for caring can be all over the map. You could care about the troops because you have a family member in the army. You could care about animals because your dog is the most important member of your family. You could care about ending hunger because you love to cook (and eat). So let's find out what you care about and put a face to that feeling in your gut.

STUFF: Pen or pencil

TIME: More time than it takes to smile, less than it takes to get into a grumpy mood

STEPS:

1. Write in your three potential Things in the blank spaces as indicated on the following pages.

2. Answer the questions for each thing by circling an emoticon. Don't think too hard—just go with your first reaction. Do this for all three rounds.

3. Compare your tests. Which Thing got you circling those big emotions (mad, happy, and shocked)? The Thing with the fewest "whatevers" is the Thing your gut is telling you to go with.

Whatever   Mad   Happy   Shocked

ROUND ONE

When I think about _____,
<span></span> <span>THING #1</span>
this is how I feel (circle one): 😐 😠 🙂 😮.

I want other people to care about

_____, and trying to make them
<span>THING #1</span>
care makes me feel (circle one): 😐 😠 🙂 😮.

When I picture myself doing something about

_____, this is how
<span>THING #1</span>
I feel (circle one): 😐 😠 🙂 😮.

ROUND TWO

When I think about _____,
THING #2

this is how I feel (circle one): 😐 😖 🙂 😮 .

I want other people to care about

_____, and trying to make them
THING #2

care makes me feel (circle one): 🙂 😖 🙂 😮 .

When I picture myself doing something about

_____, this is how
THING #2

I feel (circle one): 🙂 😖 🙂 😮 .

ROUND THREE

When I think about _____,
THING #3

this is how I feel (circle one): 😐 😖 🙂 😮 .

I want other people to care about

_____, and trying to make them
THING #3

care makes me feel (circle one): 🙂 😖 🙂 😮 .

When I picture myself doing something about

_____, this is how
THING #3

I feel (circle one): 🙂 😖 🙂 😮 .

What do you think your gut is trying to tell you? (Turn the page!)

Hey, world! Listen up!
Here is my THING (at least for now):

TAKE IT TO THE NEXT LEVEL!

DOES YOUR GUT HAVE MORE TO SAY? FORGET THE EMOTICONS AND LIST YOUR EMOTIONS OR WRITE OUT YOUR THOUGHTS IN WHOLE SENTENCES—EVEN PARAGRAPHS!

PROJECT #3: GET FOCUSED

What part of your Thing do you want to fix first? For example, if your Thing is Animal Welfare, you could focus on getting strays into shelters, or ending animal testing, or even volunteering to walk elderly people's pets. All of those would be meaningful and important actions. The challenge is to figure out which gets you most excited.

The rest of the projects in this chapter are like a treasure hunt—you're on a search for the part of your Thing that you want to do something about, the specific problem you want to solve. You're going to look through your house and neighborhood and school. You're going to comb through newspapers and magazines, and you're going to talk to a lot of people. We're going to start you off with some ideas of issues you could focus on—if one of them jumps out at you, go for it! Then, you can use the rest of the projects to find examples of your Thing in the world around you. That way, you'll really SEE IT.

STUFF: A highlighter or marker

TIME: Enough time to find your focus

STEPS:

1. On the following pages, jump to the box that features your Thing.

2. Read through the suggestions. Do they interest you? Do you want to learn more about them? Use your marker to highlight the issues that you might want to focus on.

3. Have some of your own ideas? Great! Add them to the box.

4. If you're still not sure, skim through the suggestions in the other boxes—you never know what might inspire you.

This Project is just to get your juices going. If you don't have any idea how to do this stuff, don't worry! We'll give you the info you need in Chapter 3, "Build It."

ANIMAL WELFARE

Animals feel pain, hunger, and neglect just like we do. Because they can't speak up for themselves, humans get away with abusing them, abandoning them, even killing them. Want to stand up for them? You could focus on:

1. Protecting endangered species around the world

2. Helping homeless animals in your town

3. Ending animal testing in laboratories

4. Closing factory farms and puppy mills

5. Cleaning up oceans and rivers to protect marine life

6. Other things you could focus on:

_____

_____

_____

_____

_____

DISASTER RESPONSE & RELIEF

Earthquakes, hurricanes, fires, and floods— emergencies come in all shapes and sizes. Some affect whole towns or states; some, like a fire, may just affect one family. Want to help people be prepared? You could focus on:

1. Raising awareness about the need for disaster preparedness at home, at school, and in your town

2. Helping to rebuild after major natural disasters in your town, or in other parts of the world

3. Collecting supplies for areas hit by disaster

4. Educating kids about what they can do to avoid preventable disasters like accidental fires

5. Other things you could focus on:

_____

_____

_____

_____

_____

DISCRIMINATION

What if people treated you differently because of something you couldn't change? Some people make quick judgments about other people's religion, race, weight, and disability, even whether they are a boy or a girl. Don't think that's fair? You could focus on:

1. Raising awareness about the discrimination you see in your school

2. Making sure that disabled people have access to the same things as able-bodied people

3. Making sure that girls have the same opportunities as boys

4. Fighting religious discrimination around the world

5. Other things you could focus on:

_____

_____

_____

AROUND THE WORLD: Over the past decade, about 258 million people have been affected by natural disasters worldwide.

EDUCATION

Love it or hate it, there is nothing more important  that getting a good education— but do all kids get the same opportunities in your town? Are there things about your own school that you'd like to change? If so, you could focus on:

1. Saving or protecting arts education in your school

2. Tackling overcrowding in your classrooms

3. Making sure classrooms have the supplies they need

4. Raising awareness about education inequalities in your town

5. Getting funding for after-school programs

6. Other things you could focus on:

_____

_____

_____

THE ENVIRONMENT

The environment has become a big issue in recent years. The U.S. is one of the biggest polluters in the world and this affects the air we breathe, the water we drink, and the food we eat. Want to change that? You could focus on:

1. Getting your family to recycle at home

2. Raising awareness about energy conservation at school

3. Replacing toxic chemicals used at home or in school with natural cleaning products

4. Raising awareness about global warming and alternative energies

5. Protecting animal habitats in your town or around the world

6. Other things you could focus on:

_____

_____

_____

> **SWITCH IT UP:** Alternative energy comes from unconventional sources— the sun, wind, or running water—that do not produce harmful pollution.

HEALTH & FITNESS

In the past 30 years, the number of overweight children has tripled, so staying healthy has become a big priority. Lots of people don't eat right or get exercise. Want to get people in tip-top shape? You could focus on:

1. Educating kids at school about the positive effects of physical fitness and healthy eating habits

2. Making the food healthier in your home or at school

3. Launching a campaign to get smoking banned in the areas around your school

4. Teaching people about illnesses that are caused by unhealthy lifestyles like diabetes and heart disease

5. Other things you could focus on:

_____

_____

_____

HUMAN RIGHTS

All humans should have the same basic rights: freedom to say what they want (even if it is unpopular); freedom to practice their religion; freedom from violence; and freedom from extreme poverty. Unfortunately, these freedoms aren't always protected. Want to do something about it? You could focus on:

1. Raising awareness about child labor and sweatshops

2. Fund-raising to buy mosquito nets to prevent malaria in poor countries with hot climates

3. Writing letters to free people who have been put in prison without a fair trial

4. Understanding how immigration affects the U.S. and how to protect immigrants' rights

5. Other things you could focus on:

_____
_____
_____
_____
_____
_____

POVERTY

More than one billion people live on less than $2 a day, and every minute 18 children die due to poverty-related causes (things like lack of clean water and nutritious food, bad hygiene, and limited access to doctors). Does that make you mad? You could focus on:

1. Investigating poverty rates in your town or state

2. Finding ways to donate clothes, medical supplies, and other basic goods to people in need

3. Raising awareness about how preventable diseases affect poor children around the world

4. Helping the United States meet the Millennium Development Goals (see box below)

5. Other things you could focus on:

_____
_____
_____
_____
_____

VIOLENCE & BULLYING

Every year bullying and violence affects millions of kids at home and at school. That means that chances are you or someone you know is a victim of bullying or abuse. Want to stop it? You could focus on:

1. Making people aware of the growing problem of cyberbullying

2. Drawing attention to violence at school or in your town

3. Teaching other kids to stand up for themselves against bullies

4. Campaigning for gun control in your state

5. Other things you could focus on:

_____
_____
_____
_____

MAKING POVERTY HISTORY: In 2000, 189 countries set goals to lift 500 million people across the world out of poverty by 2015. If they (we!) succeed, fewer women will die while delivering their babies, fewer people will die from preventable and/or treatable diseases, and many more kids will receive an education. The Millennium Development Goals: Reduce poverty and hunger; educate every child; provide equal chances for girls and women; reduce infant and maternal deaths; improve the health of women, especially mothers; fight diseases like HIV/AIDS and malaria; clean up the environment.

THE WARS WE'RE FIGHTING NOW:
As of 2010, over 1.6 million U.S. soldiers have served in the conflicts in Iraq and Afghanistan.

WAR & PEACE

War affects everyone: the soldiers who fight; their families back home; the people living in war zones. Want to try to find the positive in all the violence? You could focus on:

1. Supporting the troops stationed overseas and their families at home

2. Promoting peace and nonviolence

3. Raising awareness about the lives of war refugees

4. Reaching out to children living in war zones

5. Trying to end the use of child soldiers around the world

6. Other things you could focus on:

_____

_____

_____

_____

HOMELESSNESS & HUNGER

About 2 million children in the U.S. will experience homelessness each year. And over 17 million kids living in the U.S. go to bed not knowing where they're going to find their next meal. Do you want to make those huge numbers smaller? You could focus on:

1.]Hosting events for kids living in shelters

2. Making sure local food banks have the supplies they need

3. Raising awareness about homelessness and hunger in your town

4. Working to find shelter and support services for homeless veterans

5. Other things you could focus on:

_____

_____

_____

Have you figured out what part of your Thing you want to focus on? Write it here!

I'm going to focus on:

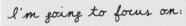

_____

_____

_____

_____

WHO IS YOUR THING?

MAYBE YOUR THING SHOWS UP IN THE BEHAVIOR OF THE PEOPLE AROUND YOU. FOR EXAMPLE, IF YOUR DAD DRINKS TEN SODAS A DAY *AND* FORGETS TO RECYCLE THE CANS, YOU'VE GOT ALL SORTS OF STUFF TO WORK WITH. HOW ABOUT SOME HEALTH AND FITNESS TIPS FOR HIM? OR WHAT ABOUT GETTING HIM TO RECYCLE?

PROJECT #4: WHERE IS YOUR WHERE?

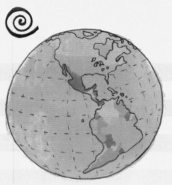

Look around your world for examples of your Thing. Is your Thing a problem in your house or apartment? In your town? Pay attention to the issues that touch your life and your community— these are great places to start making a difference.

For example, if your Thing is the Environment, figure out if you could be saving more energy at home. If your Thing is Education, find out if your school has enough funding for music and art classes. If Animal Welfare is your Thing, do you know where there are places for strays or battered animals in your town? Before you start investigating, get aware of your where!

STUFF: Pen or pencil

TIME: 10 minutes, or enough time to take in the world around you

STEPS:

1. What is your home address? Enter it in the card on the opposite page. That address defines part of your where. There is an actual building, a street, a town or city, state, and zip code. Each of those items assigns you to a community.

2. Where do you go to school? What grade are you in? These are communities, too. Fill in that info.

3. Think of other communities you belong to: your place of worship (like a church, mosque, or synagogue); a choir or other after-school clubs; a youth group; Scouts; even sports teams. There may be problems that you could fix in these communities, too.

My Where

Tear this card out and paste it on a map of the world!

My home address:

My school name and address:

My grade:

TAKE IT TO THE NEXT LEVEL!

KEEP THESE COMMUNITIES IN MIND WHEN YOU ARE OUT THERE ROCKING YOUR THING. RECRUIT THE COMMUNITY MEMBERS AND YOU COULD HAVE SOME MAJOR MANPOWER BEHIND YOU.

Other communities that I am a part of:

PROJECT #5: RATE YOUR ROOM

Your bedroom is probably the place you know best, so look for stuff in your room that might have some connection to your Thing. If you're into the Environment, your fish tank might get you thinking about cleaning up rivers, streams, and oceans. If Poverty is your Thing, you may spot a lot of stuff just lying around that people in need could actually use. If your Thing is an issue like War & Peace, look through magazines or books on your shelves that might have some interesting stories about soldiers or violent conflicts in other countries.

Beware of stinky socks!

STEPS:

STUFF: Pens or markers

TIME: 20 minutes. Unless you've got a humongous room, in which case maybe 30 minutes.

1. Sit on your bed. Draw a floor plan of your room and lay out all the different things in it—from your bedside table to the pile of clothes in the corner. It doesn't have to be exact—simple shapes will do the trick.

2. Look at the floor plan and circle the areas that are related to your Thing.

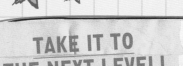

TAKE IT TO THE NEXT LEVEL!

MAP YOUR WHOLE HOUSE! IF THE ENVIRONMENT IS YOUR THING, DOES THE LEAKY FAUCET DRIVE YOU CRAZY? MAYBE WATER CONSERVATION IS YOUR FOCUS. IF HEALTH IS YOUR THING, ARE YOUR SNACK CABINETS PACKED WITH JUNK FOOD? SOUNDS LIKE YOUR PANTRY COULD USE A MAKEOVER.

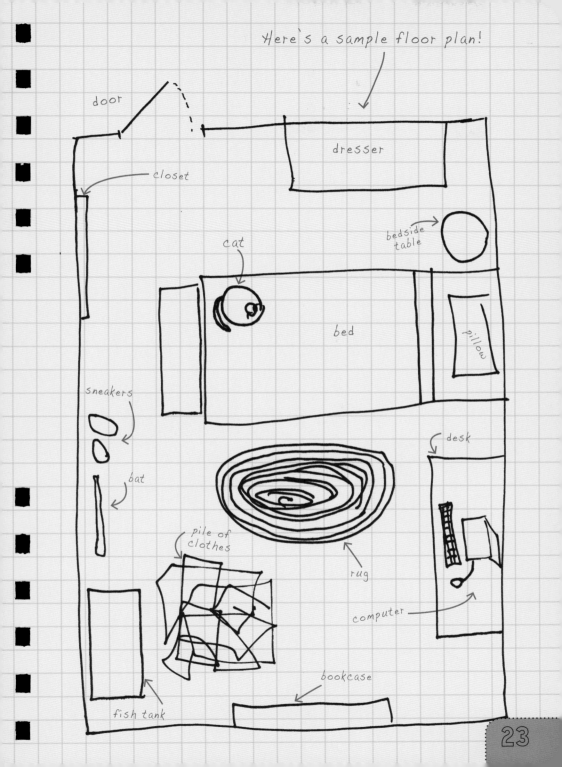

Here's a sample floor plan!

door

dresser

closet

cat

bedside table

bed

pillow

sneakers

bat

rug

desk

pile of clothes

computer

fish tank

bookcase

23

My Bedroom

My House

PROJECT #6: SCAN YOUR SCHOOL

During the day, you spend more time at school than you do at home, right? From the minute you walk out the front door of your house to the second you plop down for your after-school snack, notice what's going on around you. Do you see examples of your Thing at school? Are other kids talking about your Thing? Does your teacher bring up your Thing in the middle of class? What are they saying? Do you pass a poster or a sign about your Thing on your way home?

STUFF: Pen or marker

TIME: One school day

STEPS:

1. As you go about your school day, write down anything you see, hear, or even think about that might be related to your Thing.

2. At the end of the day, look at your notes and figure out the times when your Thing came up the most. Keep track on the notepaper below. Any more clues on what you'd like to focus on?

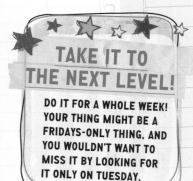

TAKE IT TO THE NEXT LEVEL!

DO IT FOR A WHOLE WEEK! YOUR THING MIGHT BE A FRIDAYS-ONLY THING, AND YOU WOULDN'T WANT TO MISS IT BY LOOKING FOR IT ONLY ON TUESDAY.

BEFORE SCHOOL   Did you get to school by car? Bus? Bike? What's the environmental impact of that daily trip?

ENGLISH

Did your teacher hand out a bunch of papers that landed in the trash (and not the recycling bin!)?

HISTORY
Did your teacher bring up current events? Anything to do with your Thing?

MATH

Are there enough textbooks to go around?

SCIENCE
Does the lab equipment seem old or out of date?

ART/MUSIC
Does everyone have all the art supplies they need?

GYM
Do you get exercise during gym or do you just hang out with your friends?

RECESS

Did you see any kids hanging out alone? Any kids having a hard time or being pushed around?

COMPUTER
Do you have a computer lab at your school? Internet access? Are kids being mean online and writing bad stuff about other kids?

LUNCH   How is lunch? Greasy and unhealthy? Is it good?

OTHER CLASSES OR ACTIVITIES   What else do you notice?

27

PROJECT #7: TAKE A HIKE

O kay, you've done your room, your home, your school. Was your Thing all over the place? Not exactly? No problem. Next up is your neighborhood! There's a lot going on out there. If your Thing is the Environment, think about pollution that might be coming from a local factory or business. If you really care about Health, pay attention to whether you're choking on cigarette smoke when you walk around your city. If Fitness is your Thing, do you see people jogging or walking? If you love animals, keep an eye out for stray dogs. If Homelessness is your Thing, do you see people who look like they're living on the streets? Your focus—the problem you want to solve—may be somewhere you pass every day, so keep those eyes open!

STUFF: Pen or marker, paper

TIME: If it's a nice day, as long as you want!

STEPS:

1. Lace up your sneakers and hit the streets to look for your Thing. (Depending on where you live, you may need a grown-up to go with you.)

2. Draw or write down anything that's related to your Thing on the opposite page.

3. If you can't walk around your neighborhood right now, take a walk in your brain. Think about the streets, schools, churches, community centers, shops, malls, or anything you pass by on a regular basis.

4. Look at your notes. Underline and circle the stuff related to your Thing. What *really* bums you out? What might you want to change or fix? Write it down at the bottom of the opposite page.

MY BLOCK   *Are people's outdoor lights on timers or do they stay on all day, wasting electricity?*

THE CENTER OF TOWN
  Is there graffiti on buildings?

THE EDGES OF TOWN
  Are there any homeless people at the bus stop or in the park?

THE SURROUNDING AREA
  Is there pollution coming from any local businesses?

MORE NOTES
What really bums you out?

TAKE IT TO THE NEXT LEVEL!

GRAB A BUDDY (OR THREE) FROM YOUR NEIGHBORHOOD AND ASK HIM WHAT THINGS HE WOULD CHANGE IF HE COULD.

Friend #1:
would change:

Write his or her name at the top

Friend #2:
would change:

Friend #3:
would change:

PROJECT #8: READ ALL ABOUT IT

Checking out the news is another great way to figure out what part of your Thing you want to focus on. Newspapers and magazines are jam-packed with information about stuff going on in your town, city, country, and world. Whatever your Thing is, it's bound to be all over those pages.

Maybe your Thing is Education and you come across a bunch of articles about your city cutting school budgets—did you even know about that? Or maybe your Thing is going on halfway across the world and examples are hard to find close to home. If your Thing is Human Rights, the international section can fill you in on countries where people's rights are threatened. Remember, the news isn't just for old people!

STEPS:

> **STUFF:** Magazines, newspapers, glue, pens or markers, scissors, tape
>
> **TIME:** A weekend morning

1. Grab your scissors, colorful pens, and some magazines and newspapers that are lying around the house. (Just make sure Mom and Dad are done with them.)

2. Flip through the articles and look for stories that have something to do with your Thing. If it's good news, make a check mark (or a smiley face); if it's bad news, mark it with an "X" (or a frowny face).

3. Once you've flipped through all your papers and magazines, it's time to compile your "research," so have your scissors and glue nearby.

4. Cut out the articles and pics that you marked up, and then cut out some key words and phrases (yep, they'll be teeny-tiny).

5. Paste these key words on the following pages, good news on the left side, bad news on the right. Paste in pics, too.

6. Answer the questions on page 34. Then write down three things you learned on page 35.

Good News :)

Bad News :(

TAKE IT TO THE NEXT LEVEL!

CUT OUT THE ARTICLE HEADLINES AND PICTURES, AND MAKE YOUR COLLAGE POSTER-SIZED. NOT ONLY WILL IT BE GREAT INSPIRATION, BUT YOU MAY BE ABLE TO USE IT TO GET OTHER PEOPLE EXCITED ABOUT YOUR THING.

The bad news is:

The bad news makes me mad because:

The good news is:

The good news makes me smile because:

Three things I learned
that I didn't know
before:

1.

2.

3.

35

PROJECT #9: GET CHATTY

Asking questions is a great way to see what bugs people and gets them thinking about what they want to change. And it might get you thinking, too. If something bugs a friend, it probably bugs someone else in your class. Maybe it even bugs you and you just haven't thought about it yet. Break out your phone or hop on Instant Messenger and ask each of your buddies to give you a couple of minutes to interview them about your Thing. We've provided you with some questions but if you think they're lame, create your own!

STUFF: Pen or pencil, paper
TIME: About 10 minutes for each conversation

STEPS:

I. Ask at least five friends the following three questions:

If I gave you $1 million to do something to fix my Thing, what would you do?

Is my Thing something you think about a lot? When you do think about it, what exactly bums you out?

What part of my Thing do you think is most important to fix first? Why?

2. As they're talking, take notes in the cards provided. You don't need to write down whole sentences. Keywords and abbreviations are good enough as long as you can understand them later.

3. If you have one, stick a picture of your friend in the box on the card to snazz it up.

4. Think about what you liked and didn't like about what your buds had to say. Did your conversation get you thinking? If you have any new ideas about what you might focus on, jot them down on the cards.

→ *Friend #1*

Name:

Answers:

Got me thinking about:

PAY TO THE
ORDER OF Keisha $ 1,000,000
One million   Dollars
Bank of Yourtown
FOR To change the world.   MP
1 6 30 26A

→ *Friend #2*

Name:

Answers:

Got me thinking about:

⟶ Friend #3

Name:

Answers:

Got me thinking about:

⟶ Friend #4

Name:

Answers:

Got me thinking about:

Paste a pic here!

→ *Friend #5*

Name:

Answers:

Got me thinking about:

TAKE IT TO THE NEXT LEVEL!

GET A DIFFERENT PERSPECTIVE. ASK A PARENT OR A FAVORITE TEACHER—THEY MAY HAVE SOMETHING NEW TO SAY.

Paste a pic here!

Grown-up

Name:

Answers:

Got me thinking about:

see it! RECAP

BY NOW YOU SHOULD HAVE A PRETTY CLEAR IDEA OF WHAT YOUR THING IS AND WHY YOU CARE ABOUT IT. IF NOT, FLIP BACK THROUGH THE PROJECTS YOU'VE DONE SO FAR. WHAT TOPICS CAME UP AGAIN AND AGAIN? WHICH PART OF YOUR THING DO YOU WANT TO FOCUS ON FIRST? WHAT'S THE PROBLEM YOU WANT TO SOLVE? REMEMBER, AFTER YOU FIX ONE THING YOU CAN ALWAYS GET STARTED ON ANOTHER! BEFORE YOU JUMP INTO THE NEXT CHAPTER, TAKE A MINUTE TO WRITE DOWN THE RESULTS OF ALL YOUR HARD WORK ON THE OPPOSITE PAGE.

My Thing is:

I'm going to focus on:

believe it!

CHAPTER 2

YOU'VE GOT A THING——A PROBLEM YOU WANT TO SOLVE. IT MAKES YOUR HEART HURT. IT MAKES YOU SQUIRMY, LIKE YOU WANT TO JUMP UP AND **DO SOMETHING RIGHT NOW!** AWESOME. THE NEXT STEP IS FIGURING OUT HOW YOU CAN CRUSH, ERASE, CLEAN, SAVE, OR CHANGE THAT THING. CARING IS GOOD. ACTION IS BETTER. **BUT BEFORE YOU CAN ACT, YOU'VE GOT TO BELIEVE,** YOU'VE GOT TO UNDERSTAND. YOU'VE GOT TO KNOW YOUR THING INSIDE AND OUTSIDE. YOU'VE GOT TO KNOW MORE THAN ANYONE. THE PROJECTS IN THIS CHAPTER WILL MAKE YOU AN EXPERT IN YOUR THING BY HELPING YOU ANSWER **SOME BIG QUESTIONS.** ONCE YOU DO, YOU'LL OWN YOUR THING. YOU'LL REALLY **BELIEVE IT.**

WHAT IS THE PROBLEM?

WHY DOES THE PROBLEM EXIST?

WHERE DID IT START?

THESE ARE THE QUESTIONS YOU NEED TO ANSWER!

DO PROJECTS #10 — #16 TO FIGURE IT OUT!

HOW BIG IS THE PROBLEM?

WHY DO I CARE ABOUT THE PROBLEM?

HOW MUCH CAN I FIX?

WHAT AM I GOING TO DO ABOUT IT?

PROJECT #10: MAP THE PROBLEM

Everything has a story. That pencil in your hand started as a tree. Your sneakers probably traveled halfway around the world from factory to store before landing on your feet. The problem you're trying to solve has a story, too.

Mapping a problem breaks an issue down into smaller pieces so you can understand it better. Once you understand it, you can come up with a great solution. You can check out the sample Problem Map on the next page, but you probably won't be able to fill it until you do the rest of the projects in this chapter. That's why a big, blank Problem Map will be waiting for you at the end of this chapter.

STUFF: Your eyes and your brain

TIME: Just a few minutes. You won't fill out your own until later.

STEPS

1. Put your pens and markers away. This is just a reading and thinking project.

2. Look over the sample Problem Map so you can get a sense of what to look for as you do the next five projects. Remember, you'll have a blank Problem Map to fill in at the end of this chapter on pages 74–75.

3. If you're already getting some ideas, jot down your notes here.

Here's a sample Problem Map:

↓

WHAT IS THE PROBLEM?

Kids in my school are unhealthy.

⬇

WHERE DOES THE PROBLEM COME FROM?

← If you want to solve a problem, you'll need to know where it comes from. You'll find answers to this one in Projects #11 and #12.

It comes from the school not giving us healthy choices at lunch.

Students never say they want a healthier lunch, so the school keeps giving us junk.

⬇

You may already know the answer to this one but you'll probably have a lot more to add as you start to learn more about the issue. ↘

WHY DO I CARE?

Because being unhealthy now means I could get sick when I'm older.

Because kids need nutritious food if they want to focus and do well in school.

→

How many dirty rivers are there in your county? How many people don't recycle in the U.S.? How many homeless people are there in your town? How many refugee camps are there in Africa? The answer to this question is not "a lot" or "a few"—it's an actual number and it's going to take some detective work. Don't worry, we'll show you how to figure it out in Projects #12, #13, and #14.

HOW BIG IS THE PROBLEM?

There are 60 kids in each grade, and four grades in my school. That means that 240 kids eat bad lunches every day.

This is your Fix-it Number and it's the first piece of your Action Plan. You'll work it out in Project #14.

HOW MUCH CAN I FIX?

I can ask the school to serve a vegetarian meal once a week.

I can pass around a petition to all 240 students to ask the school to put in a salad and veggie bar.

I can get the 20 kids in my class to write letters to the school asking for better lunches.

47

PROJECT #11: FACT SHEET 101

What's the difference between you-the-amateur-problem-solver and you-the-expert? A single piece of paper. It's called a Fact Sheet, and it's not as boring as it sounds. Your Fact Sheet is short and powerful—it shows that you know your stuff. It'll also help you convince your friends to get involved (when they see the cold hard facts about your Thing, how could they not care as much as you?), and it'll come in handy when you're spreading the word about your plans to do something.

You can't just write one up on the bus before school—a piece of paper this important has got to be well researched. We have some research tips to help you figure out where your problem comes from and how big it is. This info will also help you understand why you care so much.

STEPS:

STUFF: Pen, notebook, library card, computer with Internet access (optional)

TIME: As long as it takes for you to know your stuff!

✱ Don't stop at ten. Always take it to eleven!

1. Brainstorm at least five questions that you want to answer during your research. This will keep you on track as you dig through piles of information. Write down your questions in the space provided on page 51.

2. Make a Fact Sheet by writing the eleven most powerful and interesting facts about your Thing so they all fit on one page. Take a look at the sample Fact Sheet on page 52. We picked a general Fact Sheet on the Environment, but you could make yours more specific depending on your focus.

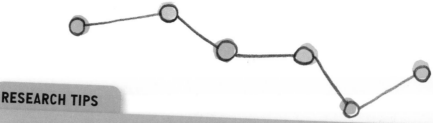

RESEARCH TIPS

BE SPECIFIC. Avoid researching broad topics like "homelessness" or "hunger." Instead, look for information on more specific things like "typical meal at a soup kitchen" or "what is the main cause of homelessness in teens?"

USE THE LIBRARY. Start with the encyclopedia. Then move to the catalog and look up your Thing by subject. Librarians don't bite, and they might have good ideas about where you can look for facts. Your school may also have accounts with major information databases like WorldBook, WebCat, ThomsonGale, and others.

SURF THE WEB. The Internet is an amazing resource, but it can be seriously overwhelming. Make sure your searches are specific (remember the first tip!) and always make sure you're using a source you can trust. Web addresses ending with .org, .gov, or .edu usually have the best information.

DON'T BE A THIEF. Don't copy down someone else's words and then use them as your own. Always keep track of where you get your info and never take chunks of text without using quotation marks. But you knew that, right? We thought so.

BE SOURCE SAVVY. Keep track of the books and websites where you found your facts. People will be impressed with the work you did, and you'll be giving credit where credit is due. And that way, when everyone gets psyched about your Thing, you can give them a bibliography full of reading material in no time.

Specific terms or phrases that will help in my research:

Great (sources) I don't want to forget:

A great source can be a website or a book packed with info—it can even be a person who was a ton of help!

50

My five good questions are:

1.

2.

3.

4.

5.

Here's a sample Fact Sheet

11 FACTS ABOUT THE ENVIRONMENT

1. Every day Americans throw out enough glass bottles and jars to fill up a giant skyscraper (think Empire State Building)!

2. The Great Pacific Garbage Patch is a 3.5-million-ton heap of debris floating in the Pacific Ocean. It is twice the size of Texas and 80% plastic! (Marine biologists say the trash found its way there through storm drains that empty out into the ocean.)

3. Plastic bags and other plastic garbage that end up in the ocean kill as many as one *million* sea creatures a year!

4. E-waste (that is, electronic waste like computers, cameras, and cell phones) are filled with highly toxic materials like lead, mercury, and cadmium. These chemicals can seep into the ground and get into the water supply if they are not recycled properly.

5. E-waste represents 2% of America's trash in landfills but is the source of 70% of our overall toxic waste.

6. The U.S. throws out approximately 300 million electronic items per year, and less than 20% of that e-waste is recycled.

7. If you replace 25% of your lightbulbs with fluorescents, you can save about 20% on your lighting bill.

8. Home refrigerators in the U.S. use the same amount of electricity as 25 large power plants every year.

9. Every year, U.S. factories spew three million tons of toxic chemicals into the air, land, and water.

10. Each year, one American produces more than 3,285 pounds of hazardous waste.

11. Over 80% of items in landfills can be recycled *but* are not.

SOURCES: Environmental Protection Agency, The New York Times, Greenpeace International

Make your own Fact Sheet!

11 Facts about:

CHECK OUT
DOSOMETHING.ORG/BOOK
FOR MORE: *blank Fact Sheet templates.*

1.

2.

3.

4.

5.

6.

7.

8.

9.

10.

11.

Sources:

PROJECT #12: ASK THE EXPERTS

Getting tired of poring over books in the library? Do your eyes hurt from staring at the computer? Before you get stuck to your chair, why don't you shake it up a bit? The best (and most fun) way to get information about your Thing is to go right to the source—the organizations or people who are trying to solve your problem, too. Just like those librarians, we promise they won't bite. They may be busy, but if you show them you're serious, you'll be surprised how helpful they can be.

To make a good impression, start every phone call, e-mail, or visit armed with thoughtful questions. You came up with some good ones in the last Project, and we'll give you a bunch more in this one.

STUFF: Pen or pencil (optional: computer, phone)

TIME: Less time than it took your problem to get so big, more time than a phone call or two

STEPS:

1. Find three organizations or people, or groups of people, that you want to talk to about your problem. (If you're not sure where to start, check out some of the organizations listed in Resources on page 275.)

2. Call them, e-mail them, or make an appointment to talk to someone in person. If you're not sure who to talk to, ask for their outreach or volunteer coordinator.

3. Use the interview log to record their answers to your questions. Don't forget to add a few of your own questions!

4. Always write a quick thank-you note to everyone you talk to. An e-mail—or better yet, a handwritten card—will go a long way in making sure that people remember you. You may need their help again! (For tips on writing a thank-you note, see Project #39 on page 250.)

INTERVIEW LOG

Date:

I interviewed:
Phone number:
Address:
E-mail address:
Do I need to call them back?   Yes _____ No _____

Why do you think this problem exists? Where does it come from?

How big is the problem?

How much are you trying to solve?

What are you doing to solve the problem?

What is your advice to other people who want to help solve this problem?

Do you have statistics, numbers, or facts that would be helpful to me?

INTERVIEW LOG

Date:

I interviewed:

Phone number:

Address:

E-mail address:

Do I need to call them back?   Yes ____ No ____

Why do you think this problem exists? Where does it come from?

How big is the problem?

How much are you trying to solve?

What are you doing to solve the problem?

What is your advice to other people who want to help solve this problem?

Do you have statistics, numbers, or facts that would be helpful to me?

INTERVIEW LOG

Date:

I interviewed:
Phone number:
Address:
E-mail address:
Do I need to call them back?   Yes ____ No ____

CHECK OUT
DOSOMETHING.ORG/BOOK
FOR MORE: ___blank___
interview logs

Why do you think this problem exists? Where does it come from?

How big is the problem?

How much are you trying to solve?

What are you doing to solve the problem?

What is your advice to other people who want to help solve this problem?

Do you have statistics, numbers, or facts that would be helpful to me?

Based on what you just learned from your research and interviews, come up with your own answers to:

Why does the problem exist?

How big is the problem?

TAKE IT TO THE NEXT LEVEL!

DID YOU TOTALLY IMPRESS ONE OF YOUR SOURCES AT AN ORGANIZATION? WAS SOMEBODY REALLY HAPPY TO HELP? ASK TO SHADOW THEM AT THEIR JOB FOR THE DAY. SPENDING A WHOLE DAY WITH SOMEONE WHO FOCUSES ON YOUR THING WILL GIVE YOU THE INSIDE SCOOP. BRING A PEN AND NOTEBOOK, OR RECORDER OR CAMERA TO CATCH EVERY STEP OF THE DAY!

Here's a sample of the note you can send —

Dear _____,

I am writing because I really admire the work you do. I'm getting involved in my community and look to you as someone I can learn from. I was hoping that you would consider letting me shadow you one day so I can learn more about the issue and what you're doing to solve it.

Please let me know if this is something you'd be willing to consider.

Best,

(Your name and contact info)

59

PROJECT #13: SURVEY CENTRAL

Asking the people in your community or school how big *they* think the problem is will help *you* figure out how big the problem is—especially if you get a lot of the same answers. The best way to collect all these answers is with a survey.

Your job: Write up a survey, hand it out, get them back, and compile the data. Yup, this is a numbers project, people. Calculators, addition, subtraction, percentages, maybe even some long division. Not a math person? Don't worry, this stuff is super-easy.

> **STUFF:** Pencil/paper (you may need that eraser), copier or printer with a computer, calculator, some patience!
>
> **TIME:** Less than an hour to make up the survey, a few days to hand out and collect the survey, and then about an hour to get all those numbers crunched. Take your time!

STEPS:

1. Model your survey after the example on the next page. Make sure you write statements that people can either agree or disagree with. Some examples:
   - *Homelessness is a big problem in our town*
   - *Schools should have music classes*
   - *Our local river should be cleaned up*

2. Stick to fewer than 10 questions—you don't want to bug people too much. Plus, the fewer questions, the more people you'll get to take the survey.

3. Hand your survey out. Ten people is okay. Twenty is better. One hundred would be AMAZING—then you'd really know what people were thinking. Collect the completed surveys.

4. Compile the data (use the box on page 62 for help).

5. After your survey is complete and you've calculated all your digits, answer the questions on page 63.

Say your Thing is getting more funding for music education in your school. Here's what a typical survey could look like. You can also make it colorful and fun —just make sure it's clear.

MUSIC EDUCATION SURVEY

PLEASE TAKE A MOMENT TO FILL OUT THIS SURVEY.
CIRCLE THE ANSWER YOU AGREE WITH THE MOST.

1. Music education is important to have in schools.

    a. Strongly agree   c. Disagree

    b. Agree   d. Strongly disagree

2. If schools need to make budget cuts, music education should be the first area to get cut.

    a. Strongly agree   c. Disagree

    b. Agree   d. Strongly disagree

3. If schools need to make budget cuts, music education should be the last area to get cut.

    a. Strongly agree   c. Disagree

    b. Agree   d. Strongly disagree

4. All kids should have access to free music classes.

    a. Strongly agree   c. Disagree

    b. Agree   d. Strongly disagree

5. How many people do you think the cuts in funding for music education affects?

    a. 20 people   c. The whole school district

    b. The whole school   d. Beyond our school district

6. Do you think this is a problem that can be addressed in a positive way?

    a. Strongly agree   c. Disagree

    b. Agree   d. Strongly disagree

7. Is there a bigger problem in our schools that should be addressed first?

    a. Yes

    b. No

    c. Cuts in music education is just as important as any other problem

    d. Cuts in music education is not a problem

HOW TO FIND A PERCENTAGE (WORKSHEET)

1. Add up the responses that you got to each statement on the survey:

How many people took your survey? _____

How many STRONGLY AGREE answers did you get? _____

How many STRONGLY DISAGREE answers did you get? _____

2. Calculate the percentage—it's easier than it sounds! To find the percentage of people who said they "Strongly Agree" with one of your statements, follow the formula in the orange box and write your own in the pink box.

| NUMBER OF PEOPLE WHO **STRONGLY AGREED** | ÷ | **TOTAL NUMBER** OF PEOPLE WHO TOOK SURVEY | × 100 = | PERCENTAGE OF PEOPLE WHO **STRONGLY AGREED** |

Now, just fill in your numbers and do the math!

_____ ÷ _____ × 100 = _____

Use the same formula to figure out the amount of people who strongly disagreed and write it in the green box.

| NUMBER OF PEOPLE WHO **STRONGLY DISAGREED** | ÷ | **TOTAL NUMBER** OF PEOPLE WHO TOOK SURVEY | × 100 = | PERCENTAGE OF PEOPLE WHO **STRONGLY DISAGREED** |

Fill in your numbers!

_____ ÷ _____ × 100 = _____

What percentage of people strongly agree with you?

What percentage of people strongly disagree with you?

Does this change the way you feel about the problem? Why or why not?

TAKE IT TO THE NEXT LEVEL!

TRY AN AWARENESS SURVEY THAT MEASURES HOW MUCH PEOPLE KNOW ABOUT AN ISSUE. ASK SIMPLE QUESTIONS LIKE "DID YOU KNOW THAT 1 IN 3 HOMELESS PEOPLE ARE UNDER THE AGE OF 18?" AND GET SIMPLE ANSWERS LIKE "YES" OR "NO." THESE SURVEYS CAN HELP YOU FIGURE OUT HOW MANY PEOPLE KNOW ABOUT PROBLEMS THAT ARE SITTING RIGHT UNDER THEIR NOSE. PLUS, YOU'LL BE TEACHING THEM SOMETHING IN THE PROCESS.

PROJECT #14: NUMBERS GAME

You know where the problem comes from—you've even figured out how big it is. Now you are going to figure out exactly how much you want (and are able) to change. We're talking real numbers here, people. It's one thing to say, "We waste a lot of energy in my house," but it would be better to say, "There are 36 lightbulbs in my house that are not energy-efficient" because it gives you a specific goal. In this case, your Action Plan could be to replace the regular lightbulbs with eco-friendly lightbulbs. That means your goal is to plug in 36 eco-friendly lightbulbs in your house.

What if your problem is harder to count? You're not off the hook—you still need to find a number. Let's say you want to tackle air pollution in your state. Start a campaign to get cars off the streets in your town. Organize a day where you get 50 kids to walk or carpool to school.

STEPS:

> **STUFF:** Pen or pencil
>
> **TIME:** Less time than it takes to count to 10,000

1. Find your Problem Number. Go back and look at your Fact Sheets, your interview log, and the surveys, and decide on a number that describes how big the problem is (say the number of icky water sources in your state, kids in your school with parents in the military, or hungry people in your city). This is your Problem Number.

2. Find your Fix-it Number. This is how much you want to change. What do you think is possible? You may not know exactly how you're going to fix the problem (that comes in the next chapter), but it's good to have a sense of how much you want to tackle. You can always go back and change this number once you start building your plan.

3. Write the two numbers down on the index cards on the opposite page so you don't forget them!

Here's a sample card

My Problem Number is: 200

This is because: there are 200 kids at a school in Uganda who don't have enough books to read.

My Fix-it Number is: 500

This is because: I want to collect 500 books to send to this school.

Now it's your turn to fill out a card!

My Problem Number is:

This is because:

My Fix-it Number is:

This is because:

THEY'RE DOING SOMETHING!

NAME: *Sarah Mathys, 11, Texas*
THING: *Disaster Relief*

SPREADING LOVE AFTER A DISASTER
Sarah lives in an area of Texas where hurricanes often leave people without shelter, food, and warm clothes. Sarah, along with her friends and school knitting club, started to knit sweaters, hats, and scarves for victims of hurricanes, which they give out at their local branch of the National Food Bank of America. Check her out at: DoSomething.org/book.

NAME: *Nick Jonas*
THING: *Diabetes*

FOR NICK, IT'S PERSONAL
In 2004 Nick Jonas found out he had type 1 diabetes. After being bummed out about his diagnosis, he decided he wanted to help other people deal with diabetes and became a role model for kids with the disease. In 2005 he went public with his diagnosis and started working with organizations like the American Diabetes Association and the Juvenile Diabetes Research Fund to help young people make healthier choices and manage their diabetes. Then he started the Change for the Children Foundation with his two bandmate brothers to raise awareness and money for diabetes research.

PROJECT #15: SUPERHERO HELP

You've been doing a whole lot of detective work: a lot of thinking, a lot of talking, a lot of searching. The Projects in this chapter have been all about the details. Take a minute to step back and think big. You're about to get out there and rock your Thing. Is there a person who inspires you? Someone who is rocking her or his own cause in an awesome way? Maybe your cousin volunteers at a home for senior citizens. Maybe your older sister taught at a fun program for kids who couldn't afford summer camp. Do your teachers donate old textbooks to schools in need? What makes your role models so great? Combine the things you admire about the people you know and create your totally perfect Superhero who will wipe all the problems of your Thing off the face of the earth.

STEPS:

1. Pick a body for your Superhero. Color it in. Design a costume for him/her.

2. Pick a mask and an emblem for your Superhero. Color it in. Or design your own from scratch! What makes your Superhero so awesome? Can he fly around the world in a minute? Is he invisible? Does he have superhuman strength?

> **STUFF:** Glue, markers, scissors
>
> **TIME:** Less time than it takes to get from the Bat Cave to Gotham City. A little longer than it takes Superman to take off into the sky.

3. Pick a tool. What does your hero do with his or her powers?

4. Cut out your mask, emblem, and tool and paste it onto your Superhero.

5. What's your Superhero's storyline? Who is he, where did he come from, and what is he doing?

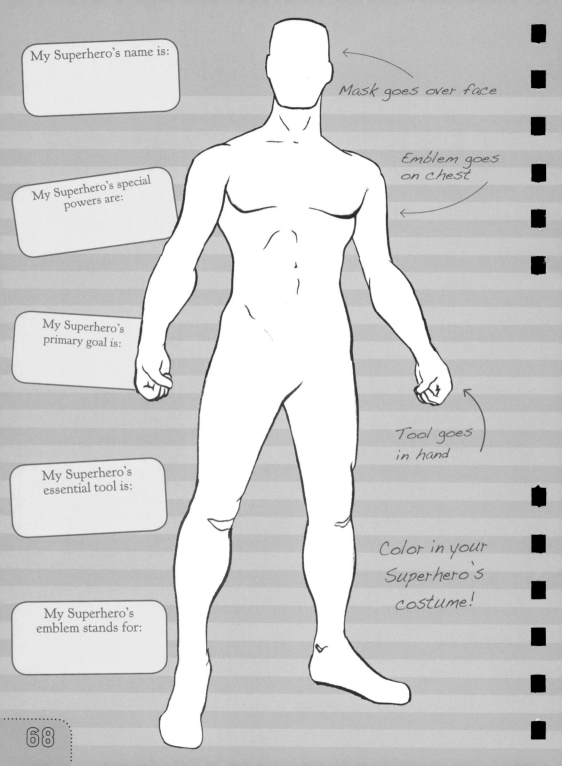

My Superhero's name is:

My Superhero's special powers are:

My Superhero's primary goal is:

My Superhero's essential tool is:

My Superhero's emblem stands for:

Mask goes over face

Emblem goes on chest

Tool goes in hand

Color in your Superhero's costume!

68

Which one of these masks best suits
your Superhero?

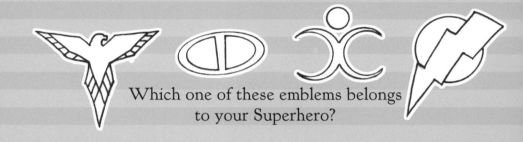

Which one of these emblems belongs
to your Superhero?

Which one of these tools does your
Superhero use?

Which one of these masks best suits
your Superhero?

Which one of these emblems belongs
to your Superhero?

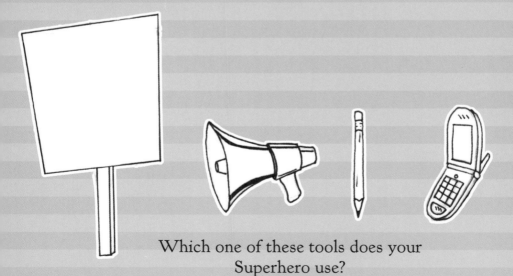

Which one of these tools does your
Superhero use?

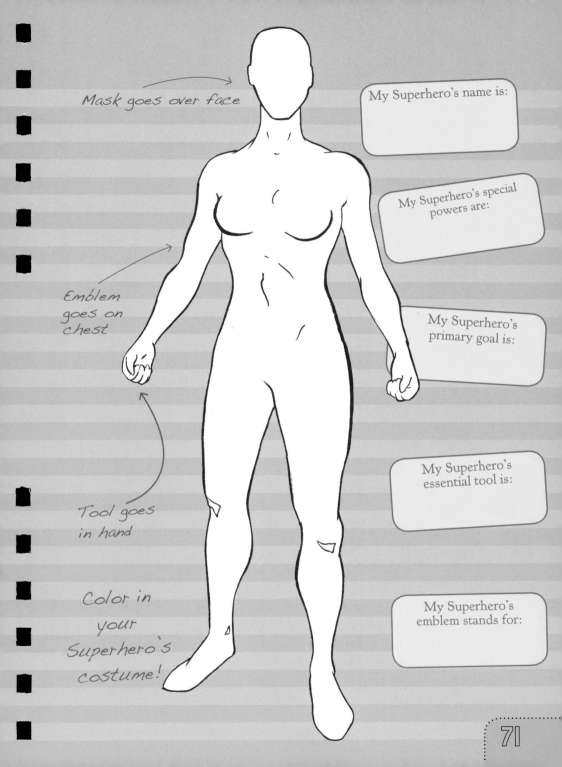

Mask goes over face

My Superhero's name is:

My Superhero's special powers are:

Emblem goes on chest

My Superhero's primary goal is:

My Superhero's essential tool is:

Tool goes in hand

Color in your Superhero's costume!

My Superhero's emblem stands for:

71

My Superhero's storyline is:

TAKE IT TO THE NEXT LEVEL!

THINK ABOUT YOUR HERO'S SUPERPOWERS.
ARE THERE ANY THAT YOU MIGHT HAVE, TOO?
MAYBE YOU CAN'T FLY AT WARP SPEED TO
DELIVER FOOD TO 1 MILLION PEOPLE, BUT YOU
COULD CONVINCE YOUR MOM TO DRIVE YOU TO
THE FOOD BANK TO HELP OUT ON A SATURDAY.

PROJECT #16: FILL OUT YOUR OWN PROBLEM MAP

You've done a lot of good work in this chapter and answered some major questions. Now it's time to get it all in one place and fill out your Problem Map. Once you've finished, tear out your Problem Map (or even better, make a supersized poster version) and post it on your wall. Whenever your Thing starts to feel too big or too overwhelming, take a look at this map to remind yourself that no problem gets solved all at once. You need to take it piece by piece, step by step.

STEPS

> **STUFF:** The projects in this chapter; a pen
>
> **TIME:** 10-15 minutes. You have all the answers already!

1. *What is the problem?* You already know this one. Flip back to page 41 where you wrote down your focus. Write it down at the top of your Problem Map.

2. *Where does the problem come from?* Take a look at the Fact Sheet you made in Project #11 on page 48. Glance over the notes you took in Project #12 on page 54. Write one or two answers in the spaces provided.

3. *Why do I care?* Even before you started researching your Thing, you knew you cared about the problem (remember the Gut Test from Project #2 on page 11?) or else you would have picked something else to focus on. But now that you're an expert, do you know why you care? Write one or two answers in the space provided.

4. *How big is the problem?* Look back at Project #14 on page 64 and fill in your Problem Number.

5. *How much can I fix?* Grab your Fix-it Number from page 65 and enter it into the map.

Fill in your own Problem Map!

WHAT IS THE PROBLEM?

WHERE DOES THE PROBLEM COME FROM?

WHY DO I CARE?

CHECK OUT
DOSOMETHING.ORG/BOOK
FOR MORE: _blank_
Problem Maps

HOW BIG IS THE PROBLEM?

HOW MUCH CAN I FIX?

11 WAYS TO BELIEVE IT

If you still don't have a handle on where your problem comes from or how big your problem is, don't worry. Jump to the card that deals with your Thing. On it are some big facts with some big numbers. Do any of them touch on the problem you want to solve?

Animal Welfare

Since 1600, more than **700** species of plants and animals have gone extinct.

Elephants that perform in circuses are often kept in chains for as long as **23** hours a day.

There are **4 - 6 million** homeless pets in the U.S.

Eighteen red foxes are killed to make one fox-fur coat, and **55** minks are killed to make a mink coat.

Disaster Relief & Response

Over the past decade, about **258 million** people have been affected by natural disasters worldwide.

A tropical storm becomes a hurricane when the speed of its winds goes over **74 mph.**

Tornadoes can form anywhere in the U.S. Their average size is about **660 feet** wide.

Floods account for about **46 percent** of disaster-related deaths in North and South America.

Discrimination

FBI Hate Crimes reports find that most racially motivated hate crimes in the United States are against African Americans.

In 2006, there were **1,305** victims of hate crimes motivated by ethnicity.

Religious intolerance is a driving force behind many of the world's armed conflicts and centers of civil unrest. Some current examples include: Protestants vs. Roman Catholics in Northern Ireland; Muslims vs. Serbian Orthodox Christians in Kosovo; Christians vs. Muslims in the Southern Philippine Islands.

Recent studies have shown that children of color who live in poor areas are more likely to attend schools filled with asbestos, live in homes with peeling lead paint, and play in parks that are contaminated.

Education

In the U.S., **1.2 million** students drop out of high school every year.

Because of budget cuts, **500,000** fewer California school children are taking music education now than they were five years ago.

Three-quarters of the nation's schools, or **59,400**, report needing repairs, renovations, or modernization in order to be declared in good condition.

Most schools in bad condition are in cities where at least **70 percent** of students live below the poverty line.

The Environment

Over the course of the year, the home refrigerators in the U.S. use the same amount of electricity as **25** large power plants.

Over **80 percent** of items that end up in landfills can be recycled.

There is a **3.5-million-ton** heap of debris floating in the Pacific Ocean that is twice the size of Texas and **80 percent** plastic.

Plastic bags and other plastic garbage thrown into the ocean kill as many as **1 million** sea creatures a year!

Health & Fitness

Every day, **30,000** Americans suffer from an asthma attack.

Over the past **30** years, the number of overweight children has doubled and the number of overweight teenagers has tripled.

In the U.S., the average adult drinks about **500** cans of soda a year. A can of soda contains 10 teaspoons of sugar.

Over **300,000** deaths in the U.S. per year are caused by diseases linked to poor nutrition and a lack of physical activity.

Homelessness & Hunger

This year, **1** in **260** runaways and homeless youths will die from assault, illness, and suicide.

Half of all young runaways left home because of a disagreement with a parent or guardian.

Feeding America, the nation's major food bank network, provides food to over **23 million** people each year.

About **96 billion** pounds of food are thrown away in the U.S. by restaurants and farmers over the course of one year.

Human Rights

There is no country in the world where women's wages are equal to those of men.

An estimated **211 million** children between the ages of 5 and 14 around the world are working.

It is estimated that there are approximately **27 million** slaves around the world.

Two-thirds of the world's children who receive less than four years of education are girls. Girls represent nearly **60 percent** of the children not in school.

Poverty

Half the world—nearly **3 billion** people—lives on less than $2 a day.

More than **800 million** people around the world go hungry each day.

In 2006, nearly **37 million** Americans lived in poverty; 12.8 million were under the age of 18.

Over **11 million** children die each year from preventable illnesses like malaria, diarrhea, and pneumonia because their families are too poor to get them the medicine they need.

Violence & Bullying

About **30 percent** of young people report being bullied, being a bully, or both.

Nearly **35 percent** of kids have been threatened online and almost one in five have had it happen more than once.

Middle school students are more than twice as likely as high school students to be affected by school violence.

Firearms are the second leading cause of death for Americans under 19.

War & Peace

Hundreds of thousands of children as young as **8 years old** around the world serve in government forces or armed rebel groups.

As of 2008, **1.6 million** U.S. soldiers have served in Iraq and Afghanistan since the conflicts began in 2001.

About **700,000** children have had a parent deployed to Iraq or Afghanistan.

There are approximately **21 million** refugees in the world fleeing violence and persecution. Nearly half of them are children.

believe it!

RECAP

YOU STARTED THIS CHAPTER KNOWING YOUR THING BUT PROBABLY NOT MUCH ELSE. HOPEFULLY NOW YOU KNOW NOT ONLY **WHAT** PROBLEM YOU WANT TO SOLVE BUT **WHY** AND **HOW MUCH**. YOU'VE DONE SOME SERIOUS RESEARCH AND YOU GOT TO PICK THE BRAINS OF SOME PRETTY INTERESTING PEOPLE. YOU EVEN DID MATH THAT WASN'T HOMEWORK. SO PAT YOURSELF ON THE BACK FOR TAKING THE TIME TO DO THE IMPORTANT PREP WORK. NOW YOU CAN HIT THE GROUND RUNNING AND BUILD AN AMAZING ACTION PLAN. TAKE A MOMENT TO RECAP WHAT YOU'VE FIGURED OUT AND THEN TURN THE PAGE!

Tear this page out of your book and stick it on a wall to remind you what you believe and why you believe it!

The problem I want to solve:

Why I care about the problem:

How much I'm going to fix:

81

build
it!

YOU'VE FIGURED OUT WHAT MATTERS TO YOU. YOU DID SOME SNOOPING AROUND AND YOU UNDERSTAND THE PROBLEM BETTER THAN ANYONE. YOU'VE EVEN CALCULATED HOW MUCH YOU'RE GOING TO FIX. SO WHAT ARE YOU GOING TO DO ABOUT IT?

THIS IS WHEN THINGS START TO GET FUN. WE'RE GOING TO START YOU OFF WITH A BUNCH OF SPECIFIC ACTION PLANS TO ROCK YOUR THING. IF NONE OF THEM FEEL QUITE RIGHT, YOU CAN INVENT A PLAN OF YOUR OWN. (WE'LL HELP YOU WITH THAT IN THE SECOND PART OF THE CHAPTER.) WHATEVER YOU DECIDE, THESE PROJECTS WILL HELP YOU BUILD IT.

THESE ARE THE QUESTIONS YOU NEED TO ANSWER!

WHAT WILL YOU DO TO ROCK YOUR CAUSE?

HOW WILL YOU PULL IT OFF?

DO PROJECTS #17 — #22 TO FIGURE IT OUT!

WHO WILL YOU WORK WITH?

WHERE WILL YOU DO IT?

HOW WILL YOU SPREAD THE WORD?

WHEN WILL YOU DO IT?

PROJECT #17: PICK A PLAN

There are so many ways to rock your Thing: from organizing a coat drive for a homeless shelter, to running a poster campaign for human rights, to getting your family to recycle. Sometimes the idea of endless possibilities can be a little scary. If you have no idea what you want to do—or even what you might be *able* to do—don't worry, we've got you covered.

We're going to start you off with a bunch of specific Action Plans that you can do to rock your Thing (32 to be exact!). There are a few suggestions for each Thing, along with the essential steps to accomplish them. There's a lot of great information in here, so even if your plan is totally mapped out in your head, you might want to flip around for some helpful hints and inspiration.

> **STUFF:** A pen
> **TIME:** How quickly can you get inspired?

STEPS:

1. Jump to the section that deals with your Thing (they're in alphabetical order); check out the suggested Action Plans. They're a surefire way to make people notice your Thing, all planned out for you!

2. If you just want pure inspiration, look through all of the Action Plans. Many of the ideas can be used as models for another project—you might be able to tweak one to fit your Thing. If your Thing is Cyberbullying, and you want to do a poster campaign, check out the MLK Day Action Plan on pages 102–103, and the plan for a Human Rights poster campaign on pages 142–143. If your Thing is Hunger and you want to do a canned-food drive, look at the collection drives Action Plans on pages 94, 108, 127, 132, and 149.

3. None of those look quite right? Jump to page 169 and get started on building your own Action Plan!

VOLUNTEER TO WALK A SHELTER DOG

Dogs need to be walked at least twice a day—including shelter dogs! If you like dogs and fresh air, offer your dog-walking services to a local shelter. Here's how:

1 FIND A SHELTER. You can do this a couple of ways:

TRY AN INTERNET SEARCH. Go to: ASPCA.ORG/ADOPTIONSHELTERS and type in your city or zip code.

TRY THE PHONE BOOK: Look up "animal shelters." Pick one that's closest to your home.

SHELTER NAME: _____

ADDRESS: _____

_____

_____

PHONE: _____

2 CHECK YOUR CALENDAR. Before you call, figure out what days you're available. If you need your parents to drive you to the shelter, be sure to check in with them.

	GOOD	BAD
MONDAYS	☐	☐
TUESDAYS	☐	☐
WEDNESDAYS	☐	☐
THURSDAYS	☐	☐
FRIDAYS	☐	☐
SATURDAYS	☐	☐
SUNDAYS	☐	☐

3 CALL 'EM UP. Here's a sample script:

"Hi, my name is [your name] and I would like to volunteer to walk some of your dogs on [date you want to walk]."

4 GET THE INFO. If they say YES, remember to ask some important questions before you hang up.

"Should I bring anything with me?"

THEIR ANSWER: _____

_____

_____

"Who should I speak to when I get there?"

THEIR ANSWER: _____

_____

_____

"What time should I come, and what time will I be finished?"

THEIR ANSWER: _____

_____

_____

If they say NO (maybe they have an age limit or too many volunteers), ask them if they know a different place where you could help out.

OTHER IDEAS: _____

NOTES: _____

5 **THE BIG DAY.** On the scheduled day, introduce yourself and tell them that you are a volunteer. Ask for the person whose name you wrote down on the previous page.

6 **WALK THAT DOG!** The shelter will probably have rules that you'll need to follow as well as some walk routes. Here are a few insider tips:

★ Stick to the sidewalks.

★ Wait for crosswalk lights to tell you to cross the street.

★ If the dog goes to the bathroom, make sure you use a plastic bag to pick up and throw away the mess.

7 **WRAP IT UP.** Return on time to the shelter and thank the employees. If you had a good time, ask if you can volunteer again!

BOYCOTT PRODUCTS THAT TEST ON ANIMALS

Every day, 38,000 animals are used to test the safety of basic products like toothpaste and shampoo. Figure out which products you use regularly that test on animals and replace them with cruelty-free versions. Here's how:

1 INVESTIGATE. Read the labels of products you use. Look for the words "cruelty-free" or the Leaping Bunny logo. This symbol means that the company has vowed not to test on animals.

If you're still not sure, visit one of these websites and look up the product by brand name.

★ LEAPINGBUNNY.ORG/SHOPPING.PHP

★ SEARCH.CARINGCONSUMER.COM

2 CHECK IT OFF. Make a checklist of the products that you use regularly.

PRODUCTS	CRUELTY-FREE?		
TOOTHPASTE	☐ yes	☐ no	☐ not sure
SHAMPOO	☐ yes	☐ no	☐ not sure
CONDITIONER	☐ yes	☐ no	☐ not sure
BODY SOAP	☐ yes	☐ no	☐ not sure
DISH SOAP	☐ yes	☐ no	☐ not sure
LAUNDRY DETERGENT	☐ yes	☐ no	☐ not sure
OTHER PRODUCTS			

3 GO SHOPPING! Tag along with a parent on their next trip to the grocery store. Bring your list and spend some time searching labels for some cruelty-free replacements. Which were you able to replace? Make a list here:

OLD PRODUCT	NEW PRODUCT

4 **MAKE AN IMPACT.** Write a letter to the company that you've decided to stop buying from and let them know that they no longer have your business. Imagine if EVERYONE stopped buying their product—then they'd have to change their ways, right?

NOTES:
_____
_____
_____
_____
_____
_____

Sample letter

To Whom It May Concern:

I have decided to stop using your product [name the product here] because your company conducts tests on animals. Animals have no voice, so they need people to stand up for them. I have switched to [name the new product] because its manufacturer has pledged that it is cruelty-free. If [name the company that makes the new product] can do it, so can you.

Sincerely,
[your name]

GIVE A PRESENTATION ON ENDANGERED SPECIES

A plant or animal species is "endangered" if it's at risk of becoming extinct. "Extinct" means it is gone for good. There are about 400 endangered animals in the United States. Raise awareness about what humans can do to protect these animals with an awesome presentation. Here's how:

BECOME AN EXPERT. Go to the public or school library and research some facts about endangered species. A simple catalog search for "endangered species" will get you a lot of great books. (Check out the box on page 49 for more research tips.)

TRY TO ANSWER THESE QUESTIONS:

What does it mean to be an endangered species?

What are some endangered species? List at least five here:

Are there any endangered species in my area?

☐ YES ☐ NO

How can animals be protected once they are considered "endangered"? Find at least three ways and list them here:

Why does it matter if animals become extinct?

_____
_____
_____
_____
_____
_____
_____
_____
_____
_____

What can humans do to protect wildlife?

_____
_____
_____
_____
_____
_____
_____
_____
_____
_____
_____
_____
_____
_____

What can I do to help right now?

_____
_____
_____
_____
_____
_____
_____
_____
_____
_____
_____
_____
_____
_____
_____
_____
_____

HAVING TROUBLE FINDING THIS INFO IN THE LIBRARY? CHECK OUT THESE WEBSITES:

★ WORLDWILDLIFE.ORG/SPECIES
★ ASPCA.ORG/ASPCAKIDS

2 FACT-CHECK. Ask your science teacher to help check your facts.

❏ FACTS LOOK GOOD
❏ NEED TO DO MORE WORK

3 **FIND YOUR AUDIENCE.** You wouldn't talk to your science class the same way you would talk to kindergartners, right? Every audience is different so be sure to figure out who your listeners are before you do too much work.

Who is this presentation for?

YOUR FAMILY	☐
YOUNGER KIDS	☐
SCIENCE CLASS	☐
WHOLE GRADE	☐
WHOLE SCHOOL	☐
OTHER	☐

4 **PLAN THE PRESENTATION.** You need to accomplish at least two things: 1. teach people about endangered species; 2. get them to care. How you go about doing that—well, that's up to you. Here is a basic presentation structure—use it as a guide, but make it your own!

PRESENTATION OUTLINE

1. Introduce yourself. Thank everyone for coming.

2. Explain what makes a species endangered. Explain what makes a species extinct.

3. Give two or three examples of endangered species (images would be really great here!).

SPECIES #1: _____
SPECIES #2: _____
SPECIES #3: _____

4. Explain why it's important to care about endangered species.

5. Give people at least two things that they can do to protect endangered species.

THING THEY CAN DO #1:
_____
_____

THING THEY CAN DO #2:
_____
_____

6. Leave time for questions. (See Project #25 on page 197 for tips.)

7. Thank everyone for coming!

5 MAKE IT FUN. Now come up with a cool way to present this information. Here are a few ideas:

Want visual aids? Make some posters with awesome pictures of endangered species.
☐ **I WANT TO DO THIS!**
☐ **NOT THIS TIME**

If you have the skills, you could make a video that mixes pictures of endangered species with strong facts.
☐ **I WANT TO DO THIS!**
☐ **NOT THIS TIME**

Feel like a game? Make a quiz to test people's knowledge about endangered species.
☐ **I WANT TO DO THIS!**
☐ **NOT THIS TIME**

Ask your principal to invite a guest speaker such as a scientist or government worker to discuss endangered species.
☐ **I WANT TO DO THIS!**
☐ **NOT THIS TIME**

Or you could do all of them!

6 SCHEDULE YOUR PRESENTATION. Talk to your teacher or the person who schedules events and decide on a day and time.

MY PRESENTATION IS ON: _____

MY AUDIENCE WILL BE: _____

7 BE PREPARED. Make sure you have all the tools you need for the presentation at least two days before the big day.

Do you have Fact Sheets to hand out? (See Project #11 on page 48.)
☐ **YES**
☐ **NO**

Will you need a microphone?
☐ **YES**
☐ **NO**

Will you need a slide or video projector?
☐ **YES**
☐ **NO**

ANYTHING ELSE?

_____
_____
_____
_____
_____
_____
_____
_____
_____

8 THE BIG DAY. You've covered all the details and you're super-prepared. You may have some butterflies in your stomach, but don't worry—you're going to be great!

HOLD A TOY DRIVE FOR DISASTER VICTIMS

Many disasters and fires leave people with nothing. Families have to buy important things like food, furniture, and hygiene products, so toys are usually the last thing they replace. You can help by organizing a toy drive for children affected by a disaster or fire. Here's how:

1 GET THE FACTS. Scan the local newspaper to find stories on recent disasters. Head to the library or the Internet and find out the following information (check out the box on page 49 for research tips):

WHAT HAPPENED IN THE DISASTER?

_____
_____
_____
_____

WHERE WAS THE DISASTER?

_____
_____
_____
_____

HOW MANY PEOPLE WERE AFFECTED?

_____

HOW MANY OF THOSE PEOPLE WERE KIDS?

_____

2 FIND A PLACE TO DONATE. Once you collect the toys, you'll need someone to distribute them.

Your local fire department will often distribute toys. (Don't dial 911! Look them up on the Internet or in the yellow pages.) Tell them that you want to hold a toy drive and ask them if they'll help.

FIRE DEPARTMENT PHONE NUMBER:
_____
CONTACT NAME:
_____

OR, you can call your local chapter of the Red Cross.

PHONE NUMBER:
_____
CONTACT NAME:
_____

I AM GIVING THE TOYS TO:

ORGANIZATION NAME:
_____
CONTACT NAME:
_____
PHONE NUMBER:
_____

3 GET THE GREEN LIGHT. Ask your principal if you can host a toy drive at school. Be sure to tell him or her why. (Get that Elevator Pitch from Project #24 on page 193.)

☐ THE PRINCIPAL SAID YES
☐ THE PRINCIPAL SAID NO. THE REASONS HE/SHE GAVE:
_____
_____
_____

If he/she said no, don't be discouraged. Here are some other places you could hold a drive:

* Community center
* Place of worship
* Town hall
* YMCA

4 GET YOUR TEACHERS ON BOARD. After each of your classes, ask the teacher if they'll do something crazy if you reach a certain goal, like promise to wear a ridiculous T-shirt to work or shave their heads.

MY TEACHERS ARE GOING TO HELP BY:
_____
_____
_____
_____
_____
_____
_____
_____
_____
_____
_____

5 GET YOUR FRIENDS ON BOARD. You could do this on your own, but everything is more fun with friends. Get some helpers!

Helper #1's Name:
Contact Info:
Responsibilities:

Helper #2's Name:
Contact Info:
Responsibilities:

Helper #3's Name:
Contact Info:
Responsibilities:

*Need more room? Flip to page 268.

6 SET THE DATES. Decide how long your drive will run. A week is good. Two weeks is even better! Any longer than that, and people might start to lose interest.

The drive will start on:

The drive will end on:

Disaster Relief

7 LOCATION, LOCATION, LOCATION. Figure out where you want to place the collection bins. Areas with heavy foot traffic work the best.

I'M GOING TO PUT BINS IN THE FOLLOWING PLACES:

❑ School entrances and exits
❑ In the cafeteria
❑ Outside the auditorium
❑ Other locations:
_____
_____
_____
_____

8 GET YOUR BOXES. Have everyone search their homes for large cardboard boxes. Ask the principal's office or your teachers if they have boxes to spare. Decorate them with glitter and paint so they pop!

9 SPREAD THE WORD. The more people who know about the drive, the more donations you'll get. Make posters and flyers announcing the drive at least two weeks in advance. (Check out Project #30 on page 216 for tips.) Make sure the poster has the following information:

★ **TOY DRIVE** in big letters at the top

★ What happened

★ Where it happened

★ How many people were affected

★ Dates of the toy drive

★ Drop-off locations

★ What kind of toys you're collecting

10 USE YOUR LUNGS. Ask if you can say something during morning announcements or homeroom. Or just use your big mouth during lunch or in between periods and shout out the cause. It could sound something like this:

11 GET YOUR TEACHERS ON BOARD. Ask your teachers if they'll agree to do something crazy if you reach a certain goal, like promise to wear a ridiculous T-shirt to work or shave their head.

12 MAKE A GOAL. Set a goal for the amount of toys you want to collect and update the sign every day with the amount collected and the amount still to go.

MY GOAL IS TO COLLECT _____ TOYS!

★Ask if you can put the poster in the school office or a place where everyone passes.

★Ask teachers to write the goal on their chalkboards so no one forgets!

13 CLOSE DOWN. Officially end the drive by announcing the amount of donations collected. Write a special thanks to everyone who helped out! (See Project #39 on page 250 for great ways to say thank you.)

WHO NEEDS TO BE THANKED?

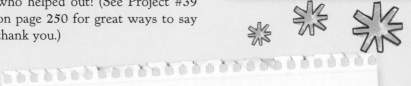

"Listen up!

[Name of disaster] affected [number of victims], including young kids.

We're helping out by holding a toy drive on [days of drive]. Just drop off your new or used toys in the boxes [list locations]. Let's put a smile on these kids' faces!"

Disaster Relief

97

HOLD A BAKE SALE TO RAISE MONEY FOR DISASTER VICTIMS

When natural disasters affect an entire community, donating money is often the best way to help. Why not hold a bake sale? You'll be able to raise awareness about the disaster and raise a wad of cash at the same time. Here's how:

1 GET INFORMED. Head to the library or, if the disaster just happened, grab the local paper and scan the headlines for articles about the disaster. (You can make a cool good news/bad news chart like the one in Project #8 on pages 32–33.)

2 FIND AN ORG. You'll need to send the donation to an organization working with the victims. If the newspaper doesn't mention any organizations collecting donations, it's likely that the local chapter of the American Red Cross is doing something to help.

★ Go to WWW.REDCROSS.ORG and type in your zip code to get their contact information.

THE DONATIONS WILL GO TO:
_____
_____
_____
_____
_____
_____

3 GET THE OKAY. Ask your principal if you can host a bake sale at school. Tell them some facts about the disaster and explain that you want to raise money for the victims. (Grab your Elevator Pitch from Project #24 on page 193.)

☐ **THE PRINCIPAL SAID YES**
☐ **THE PRINCIPAL SAID NO. THE REASONS HE/SHE GAVE:**
_____
_____
_____
_____

If he or she said no, don't be discouraged. Here are some other places you could hold a bake sale:

★ Community center
★ Place of worship
★ Town hall
★ YMCA

4 SCHEDULE IT. Discuss with your principal the best times to sell your goodies (we think lunchtime would be the smartest).

DAY	TIME

5 **LOCATION, LOCATION, LOCATION.** Set up your table in an area where there's a lot of foot traffic.

  * By the main entrance
  * In the cafeteria
  * By the basketball hoops
  * Other locations:

_____

6 **SPREAD THE WORD.** Put up flyers or make a morning announcement with the following information (check out Project #30 on page 216 for tips):

  * BAKE SALE in big letters at the top

  * What the disaster was, when and where it happened

  * How many people were affected

  * What these people need

  * Name of organization you are supporting

  * The dates and location of the bake sale

7 **DECIDE WHAT TO SELL.** Ask your friends to volunteer to make one or two goodies. Make sure you have variety!

VOLUNTEER	WILL BE MAKING

8 **PRICE IT OUT.** Don't price your items too high, or kids won't want to buy them (try 50¢ to $1 per item). Make a price list here:

GOODIE	PRICE

9 **GET SOME HELPERS.** Hopefully you'll have too many customers to handle by yourself so ask a few friends to help you out at the table.

Helper #1's Name:

Contact Info:

Responsibilities:

Helper #2's Name:

Contact Info:

Responsibilities:

Helper #3's Name:

Contact Info:

Responsibilities:

*Need more room? Flip to page 268.

10 **GET ORGANIZED** Here's what you'll need:

❑ stickers for prices

❑ baggies for individual treats

❑ calculator

❑ napkins

11 **SET UP A TABLE.** Have everyone bring their treats at least 10 minutes before the bake sale starts. Some other tips:

★Make sure everything is ordered and on display. And that prices are easy to see!

★As people buy the food, put the money you make in a lock-box, pencil pouch, or a bag with a seal or zipper.

★ Keep the money safe in your locker or have a teacher lock it up in the classroom.

12 **DONATE.** Here's the fun part— sending the money to the people who need it! The easiest way would be to give a grown-up the cash and have them write a check. Then you can mail the donation to your organization of choice. Contact the org or visit their website to find out:

WHO THE CHECK SHOULD BE MADE OUT TO:

ADDRESS WHERE THE CHECK SHOULD BE MAILED:

CREATE AN EVACUATION PLAN FOR YOUR HOME

You probably do fire drills at school, but have you ever done one at home? Making a good evacuation plan for your family may not seem like changing the world but it will make a difference in your family. And sometimes that's the best place to start. Here's how:

1 MAKE A LIST. List all of the exits in your home (this includes windows!).

_____
_____
_____
_____
_____
_____
_____
_____
_____
_____
_____
_____
_____
_____
_____

2 MAKE A MAP. Draw a map of the ground floor of your house. Pick a bright color and mark all the exits with an X. Mark each type of exit with a special color (blue for doors, red for windows, etc.).

3 MEET UP. Hold a family meeting to discuss the evacuation plan. You'll need to decide:

Who is responsible for younger siblings?
_____

Who is responsible for grandparents?
_____

Who is responsible for pets?
_____

Where will everyone meet afterward?
PLACE #1 (outside your house or building):
_____

PLACE #2 (a friend or relative's house, in case your entire neighborhood is evacuated):
_____

Who will you call once you are safe?

NAME:
PHONE:
_____

4 RUN A DRILL. Surprise everyone with a fire drill. Use a stopwatch and time how long it takes everyone to evacuate the house and get to the meeting place.

HOW LONG DID IT TAKE?
_____

COULD YOU DO IT FASTER? TRY IT AGAIN!

5 DISPLAY IT. Hang your exit map and the evacuation plan on the fridge so your family will see it.

MAKE POSTERS FOR MARTIN LUTHER KING DAY

Martin Luther King Jr.'s powerful words continue to inspire those fighting for equal rights regardless of race, gender, ethnicity, religion, or disability. Spread Dr. King's message of tolerance with a poster campaign. Here's how:

1 GET PERMISSION. Ask a teacher or someone who works at the principal's office if you are allowed to post your signs around school. Tell them you want to hang posters with quotations from Dr. King. (Check out Project #24 on page 193 for tips on making a great Elevator Pitch.)

2 FIND POWERFUL WORDS. Dr. King was known for giving amazing speeches, so it shouldn't be too hard to find some great quotations. Look in the library's biography section for a book written about him or head to the reference section and look his name up in a big book of quotations such as *Bartlett's Familiar Quotations*.

HERE ARE SOME OF OUR FAVORITES:

"Let no man pull you low enough to hate him."

"The time is always right to do right."

"I have a dream that one day this nation will rise up and live out the true meaning of its creed: 'We hold these truths to be self-evident, that all men are created equal.'"

"Injustice anywhere is a threat to justice everywhere."

"We must meet the forces of hate with the power of love."

OTHER QUOTES I LOVE:

_____
_____
_____
_____
_____
_____
_____

3 FIND IMAGES. Sometimes pictures make stronger statements than words. What images could make your message pop?

* Pictures of Martin Luther King Jr.
* Photos from civil rights marches of the 1950s and 1960s
* Images of kids of different races, genders, religions, ethnicities, and disabilities

OTHER GREAT IMAGES I COULD USE:

_____
_____

4 GET THE MATERIALS. You may already have the supplies lying around the house. If not, ask your art teacher to donate some materials. If you're feeling brave, ask the manager at an art supply store if he/she will

Discrimination

donate the material. (Remember that Elevator Pitch!)

SUPPLIES:
- ❏ Poster board
- ❏ Colorful markers
- ❏ Poster paint
- ❏ Masking tape
- ❏ Other
_____
_____
_____

PEOPLE I CAN ASK TO DONATE MATERIALS:
_____
_____
_____

5 **BUILD A TEAM.** Get your friends on board to help you out.

Helper #1's Name:

Contact Info:

Responsibilities:

Helper #2's Name:

Contact Info:

Responsibilities:

Helper #3's Name:

Contact Info:

Responsibilities:

Need more room? Flip to page 268.

6 **ONE LAST OKAY.** Show the finished posters to the person who gave you permission earlier. After they okay it, you and your friends can start posting.

7 **TIMING IS EVERYTHING.** Martin Luther King Day is the third Monday in January, so plan to put up the posters about a week before the holiday. If you can't wait until next January, do it now! Every day is a good day to celebrate Dr. King!

NOTES:
_____
_____
_____
_____
_____
_____
_____
_____
_____
_____
_____
_____
_____
_____
_____
_____
_____
_____
_____
_____
_____
_____
_____
_____
_____
_____

Discrimination

LEAD A DISCRIMINATION EXERCISE

Discrimination

Sometimes the best way to understand a complicated issue is to experience it firsthand. This exercise will give your classmates a taste of what it feels like to be discriminated against.

1 SCHEDULE IT. Explain to your teacher what you want to do. (You can even show him or her this guide.) Then, the two of you can look at the schedule and get it on the calendar. You'll need about an hour total—30 minutes for the game and at least 20 minutes for the class discussion. (Do they need convincing? Use your Elevator Pitch from Project #24 on page 193.)

DAY I WILL DO THE EXERCISE:

_____

2 GET STARTED. To begin the exercise, divide your class into groups based on physical traits. Some good ideas are:
* Hair color
* Eye color
* Shoe size
* Braces/No braces
* Other: _____
* Other: _____
* Other: _____
* Other: _____

3 Inform each group what rules or privileges they have for the next hour. For instance:

* If you're in class, let one group have free time while everyone else has to do math worksheets.

* If you can go outside, organize a game of Tag or Capture the Flag and make one group sit out.

EXAMPLE OF WHAT TO SAY:

> Okay! All the kids with braces can play Capture the Flag. All the kids who don't have braces have to sit out and be quiet. Sorry, that's just the way it is.

4 REFLECT IT. After the 30 minutes is up, go to the front of the class and ask your classmates the questions on the next page. (Remember, you need at least 20 minutes for the discussion; this might mean you have to stop the game early.)

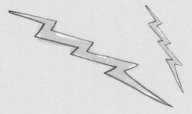

1. How did it feel to be in the group that couldn't participate?

2. How did it feel to be in the group that had fun?

3. Did you think it was fair that some groups got to do things just because they have a different physical trait?

4. Did the exercise change the way you think about discrimination?

5. What are some things you could say the next time you see someone excluded because of the way they look or because they might be different?

5 **TAKE NOTES.** Write the responses on the chalkboard so everyone can see. Ask your teacher or a friend to copy the answers down on paper. Make copies to hand out so no one forgets the important lessons of the exercise.

Discrimination

ORGANIZE A READING FOR BLACK HISTORY MONTH

To be discriminated against is to have your voice silenced. Celebrate the voices of African Americans by holding a poetry reading for Black History Month (in February). If you've never been to a poetry reading before, don't worry, it's pretty simple. Here's how you throw one:

1 FIND YOUR VOICES. A poetry reading is like a music recital—instead of playing instruments, people read a favorite poem or one that they wrote themselves. You'll need to figure out when and where you'll host the reading, but why not start with the fun part—figuring out what people could read.

Head to the library and check out some poetry books by African American poets.

You could start with some of these:

- ★ *Brown Honey in Broomwheat Tea,* by Joyce Carol Thomas

- ★ *Hip Hop Speaks to Children: A Celebration of Poetry with a Beat,* edited by Nikki Giovanni

- ★ *Poetry for Young People: Maya Angelou,* edited by Dr. Edwin Graves Wilson

- ★ *Poetry for Young People: Langston Hughes,* edited by David Roessel and Arnold Rampersad

Other great poets to explore:

- • Amiri Baraka
- • Rita Dove
- • Paul Laurence Dunbar
- • Claude McKay

2 PICK A POETIC PLACE. You want to find a place that is big enough to fit a lot of people, but isn't so big that voices will get lost. Try:

- ★ A classroom (your English teacher might be really into this idea)
- ★ Your school's library or auditorium
- ★ A community center
- ★ Your town hall
- ★ A local café

I WANT TO HOST MY POETRY READING AT:

_____

_____

_____

IF THAT DOESN'T WORK OUT, THEN I'LL TRY:

_____

_____

_____

3 SCHEDULE IT. Visit the space and ask for the person in charge of events. Before you approach them, make sure you have your Elevator Pitch ready from Project #24 on page 193. Be sure you discuss:

- * When you would like to host it (you'll need to find a time that works for both of you)
- * How many people you would like to invite (confirm that the space isn't too big or too small)

4 GO, TEAM, GO. Get a bunch of friends or family to volunteer to read a favorite poem. Keep track of who is reading what:

READER'S NAME	POEM THEY WILL READ

5 HYPE IT UP! Hang up big, bright posters announcing your event. If you're having it at school, hang posters in the halls and lunchroom. If you're having it at a coffee shop or rec center, hang them up around town.

THE POSTERS SHOULD INCLUDE:

- ★ Date and time of reading
- ★ Where the reading will take place
- ★ Who can come (Students only? Parents? Anyone?)
- ★ Anything else? (Providing snacks? Let them know!)

Check out Project #30 on page 216 for poster-making tips.

6 GO WITH THE PROGRAM. Make a pamphlet or program to hand out to audience members. Include:

- ★ The order of readers and the poems they'll be reading
- ★ Some facts about Black History Month. If you found any facts about discrimination or the civil rights movement, include them here.
- ★ Short biographies of the poets whose work you will be reading. (Check out the box on page 49 for some research tips.)

7 OPEN THE SHOW. It's up to you to introduce each reader before their turn. (If you don't feel comfortable at the microphone, ask a fearless friend to be the host.) Your intro can sound something like this:

Thank you for coming. We organized this poetry reading to honor the voices of African American poets and to send the message that everyone's voice deserves to be heard. We hope you enjoy it!

Discrimination

HOLD A SCHOOL-SUPPLY DRIVE

Back-to-school time can be tough for low-income families who can't afford to buy school supplies. Help these families by organizing a school-supply drive. Here's how:

1 CHOOSE A SCHOOL. Contact a few schools in your area to find one that will accept donated supplies. Ask the main office of your school for a list of local schools and contact information.

School Name: _____
Number: _____
Contact Person: _____

School Name: _____
Number: _____
Contact Person: _____

School Name: _____
Number: _____
Contact Person: _____

School Name: _____
Number: _____
Contact Person: _____

School Name: _____
Number: _____
Contact Person: _____

2 PREP FOR THE CALL. Before you call, figure out what you're going to say. It could be something like:

> "Hi, my name is [your name] and I go to [name of school]. I'm calling because I'd like to have a school-supply drive and want to know if you're interested in receiving the donated supplies."

If they say **YES**, ask what school supplies they need and be sure to make a list of them.

THEY NEED:

NOTEBOOKS	☐ YES	☐ NO
PENCILS	☐ YES	☐ NO
PENS	☐ YES	☐ NO
ERASERS	☐ YES	☐ NO
FOLDERS	☐ YES	☐ NO
BINDERS	☐ YES	☐ NO
MARKERS	☐ YES	☐ NO
CRAYONS	☐ YES	☐ NO
RULERS	☐ YES	☐ NO
PROTRACTORS	☐ YES	☐ NO
CALCULATORS	☐ YES	☐ NO
BACKPACKS	☐ YES	☐ NO

OTHER THINGS:
_____
_____

3 THINK BIG. If no school near you is accepting donations, ask at churches, temples, or community centers.

ORGANIZATION: _____
PHONE NUMBER: _____

4 GET THE OKAY. Ask the principal if you can host a school-supply drive. Explain why, but keep it simple. (Don't forget your Elevator Pitch from Project #24 on page 193.) Be sure to include all the details including:

WHO I'M COLLECTING FOR:

_____
_____
_____

WHAT I'M COLLECTING:

_____
_____
_____

5 SET THE DATES. Decide how long your drive will run. A week is good. Two weeks is even better! Any longer than that, people might start to lose interest.

THE DRIVE WILL RUN FROM _____
TO _____

6 LOCATION, LOCATION, LOCATION. Figure out where you want to put the collection boxes. Places with heavy foot traffic work the best.

I'M GOING TO PUT BOXES IN THE FOLLOWING PLACES:

❑ School entrances and exits
❑ In the cafeteria
❑ Outside the auditorium

Other places:

_____
_____
_____

7 GET YOUR TEACHERS ON BOARD. Ask your teachers if they'll agree to do something crazy if you reach a certain goal, like promise to wear a ridiculous T-shirt to work or shave their heads.

HOW WILL YOUR TEACHER HELP?

_____
_____
_____

8 BUILD A TEAM. You could do this on your own, but everything is more fun with friends. Get some helpers! List their names and contact info here:

Helper #1's Name:
Contact Info:
Responsibilities:

Helper #2's Name:
Contact Info:
Responsibilities:

Helper #3's Name:
Contact Info:
Responsibilities:

*Need more room? Flip to page 268.

Education

9 **GET YOUR BOXES.** Have everyone search their homes for large cardboard boxes. Also ask the principal's office or your teachers if they have boxes to spare. Decorate the boxes with paint and glitter so they pop!

10 **SPREAD THE WORD.** The more people who know about the drive, the more donations you'll get. Make posters and flyers ahead of time giving people the details. Make sure the poster and flyers have the following information (check out Project #30 on page 216 for more tips).

* SCHOOL-SUPPLY DRIVE in big letters

* The days of the drive

* What you are collecting

* Where the students should drop off supplies

* Whether or not the items need to be new

11 **USE YOUR LUNGS.** Ask if you can say something during morning announcements or homeroom. Or just use your big mouth during lunch or in between periods and shout out the cause. It could sound something like this:

"Listen up! Do you have all the pencils, crayons, notebooks, and backpacks you need? Not everybody does. Some families in our town have a hard time getting school supplies for their kids. We're helping out by hosting a school-supply collection drive on [days of drive]. Just drop off supplies like [what is needed] in [collection box locations]. Let's show people we care!"

12 **MAKE A GOAL.** Thirty notebooks? 100 pens? 60 packs of crayons? Set some goals and update a poster every day with the latest amount.

* Put the poster in a place where everyone passes.

* Ask teachers to write the numbers on their chalkboards.

MY GOAL IS TO COLLECT

13 **CLOSE DOWN.** Officially end the drive by placing your poster with the final amount of donations in the main lobby or lunchroom. Write a special thank you to everyone who chipped in! (See Project #39 on page 250 for thank-you note tips.)

14 **GET IT TOGETHER.** Get your friends to help put the supplies in bags for drop-off. Make the sorting process easier by putting pencils in one bag, crayons in another, etc.

15 **CONTACT THE SCHOOL OR ORG.** Tell them you're ready to drop off the supplies. Schedule a time and a day. Make sure you have a ride if you need one!

DROP-OFF TIME: _____

WHO'S GOING TO TAKE ME? _____

NOTES: _____
_____
_____
_____
_____
_____
_____
_____
_____
_____
_____
_____
_____
_____
_____
_____
_____
_____
_____
_____
_____
_____
_____
_____
_____
_____
_____
_____
_____
_____
_____
_____
_____
_____
_____
_____
_____
_____
_____
_____

ORGANIZE AN ART EXHIBIT

Even if you love school, you probably wish you could change some things. If you and your friends have something to say, why not say it through art? Set up an art show so teachers, parents, and siblings can see what you guys see. (If your school needs to green it up, take photos of kids recycling or design a cool recycle logo.) Here's how:

| FIND THE SPACE. You want a place with a lot of wall space and good light.

If you're doing it in school, think:
* Gym
* Library
* Hallways

If it is for the entire community, think:
* Public library
* Coffee shop or a café

2 BUILD SUPPORT. If you're hosting the show at your school, get your teachers on board first, then go with them to the principal to get it all approved. Art teachers may be willing to dedicate a class period to create art for your show—just ask! You'll also need to recruit a few friends to help you spread the word and set things up the day of the show.

TEACHERS ON BOARD:

FRIENDS ON BOARD:

Name:

Contact Info:

Responsibilities:

Name:

Contact Info:

Responsibilities:

Name:

Contact Info:

Responsibilities:

3 FIGURE OUT THE DETAILS. What kind of art can people submit?

PHOTOGRAPHS	☐ YES	☐ NO
PAINTINGS	☐ YES	☐ NO
VIDEO ART	☐ YES	☐ NO
COMICS	☐ YES	☐ NO
SCULPTURE	☐ YES	☐ NO

OTHER KINDS:

Education

Are there certain rules about subject matter?

❑ YES ❑ NO

If so, what are they?

Can anyone enter the show?

❑ YES ❑ NO

What is the deadline for entries?

DEADLINE:

4 **CALL FOR SUBMISSIONS.** Make an announcement at school or send out an e-mail. It could sound something like this:

> Hey guys, if you could change anything about school, what would it be? Take your idea and turn it into an awesome piece of art. We'll put it on display so you can tell the world what you think!

WHO'S INTERESTED? LIST THEIR NAMES:

_____
_____
_____
_____
_____

5 **ADVERTISE!** Make flyers and posters. Get an artist friend to help make them look great (it shouldn't be hard, it is an art show!). Check out Project #30 on page 216 for tips on making a flyer. Be sure it includes:

> ★ART SHOW at the top
>
> ★What the art show is all about
>
> ★When the art show will be
>
> ★Where it will be

6 **MAKE A STATEMENT.** Ask all the participating artists to write a short (think three sentences!) statement about what they'd like to see change at school and how they've shown that in their art. Hang the statements next to their artwork.

7 **MAKE A PROGRAM.** Pass out programs to people who come to the exhibit. Let them know:

* The names of all the artists
* The theme of the show and why it's important

Education

113

WRITE A LETTER TO THE SCHOOL BOARD ASKING FOR MORE ARTS PROGRAMS

Arts programs are usually the first thing to be eliminated when schools are making budget cuts. Does that bum you out? Write a letter to the school board! Yes, we said it. You've probably heard a bazillion times from teachers and just about anyone who hears you complain about something in your community: "Why don't you write a letter?" Well, now we are saying it too: write a letter! People will listen.

1 GET NAMES. The school board makes the budget decisions for your school district. Ask the school secretary for the address and the names of all the board members.

MEMBER NAMES:

_____
_____
_____
_____
_____
_____

SCHOOL BOARD ADDRESS:

_____
_____

2 ADDRESS IT. Write a letter to each board member individually. Address them as "Ms." and "Mr." If you're not sure whether the person is a man or woman, address the letter "Dear School Board Member [full name]."

3 CHECK OUT THESE TIPS.

* Decide if you want to type or write the letter by hand. Don't underestimate the power of a handwritten letter; it will stand out from the piles of faxes and e-mails school board members receive daily.
* Keep it short and to the point.
* Be polite; don't be too aggressive.

4 MAKE YOUR CASE. Facts carry a lot more weight than reasons like "because it's important." So, get some facts together about the value of arts education. For example:

FACT 1: Musical training has been found to improve how the brain processes the spoken word. This finding could help the reading ability of children with dyslexia or other reading problems.

FACT 2: Students in the arts are found to be more cooperative with teachers and peers, more self-confident, and better able to express their ideas.

FACT 3: Children who study music and the arts have higher grades, score better on standardized tests, have better attendance records, and are more active in community affairs than other students.

Check out *DoSomething.org/book* or *VH1SaveTheMusic.com* for more facts.

5 **BE SPECIFIC.** The school board deals with a lot of problems every day, but if members see that you have a particular problem or issue in mind, then it'll be easier for them to take action to resolve it. For example:

"I'm writing because the arts programs are being cut in my school. I am asking that you please reverse the decision to cut our music classes."

6 **WRAP IT UP.** Thank them for their time and consideration and sign your name.

7 **BE YOURSELF.** You should follow the basic rules of a formal letter, but make sure the letter sounds like you. The more honest and passionate you sound the more effective your message will be.

NOTES:
_____
_____
_____
_____
_____
_____
_____
_____
_____
_____
_____
_____
_____
_____
_____
_____
_____
_____
_____
_____

START RECYCLING AT HOME

Tired of seeing your parents toss soda cans and newspaper into the regular garbage? Wish they would recycle? Here's how to get them on board:

1 THE RULES. Contact your local recycling center and figure out the recycling rules for your town.

★ **TRY A WEB SEARCH.** To find your local recycling center, go to **EARTH911.ORG** and enter your zip code. Or, go to **GOOGLE.COM** and type in the name of your town and "sanitation" or "trash collecting."

★ **CHECK THE PHONE BOOK.** Most yellow pages have a section in the front that lists important numbers, including sanitation or recyclying. Call them up and ask to speak to the recycling coordinator.

PHONE NUMBER: _____

2 GET THE WHAT. Find out what kinds of materials your town will recycle.

LIST THEM HERE: _____
_____
_____

3 GET THE HOW. Find out how the recycling should be organized.

Place in a special trash can
❏ YES ❏ NO

Place in a clear plastic bag
❏ YES ❏ NO

Place in separate plastic and paper
❏ YES ❏ NO

4 GET THE FACTS: You'll need some ammunition to convince your family that recycling is important. Make a Fact Sheet on the environmental impact of recycling. (Check out Project #11 on page 48 for instructions on making a killer Fact Sheet.)

5 GET 'EM TOGETHER. Call a family meeting and be sure to bring:

★ Your town's recycling guidelines

★ Your Fact Sheet and any other material you think might help to convince them.

6 MAKE A PLAN. Once you get the family on board, you can discuss:

WHERE WILL WE KEEP THE RECYCLING?
In the kitchen ❏ YES ❏ NO
In the garage ❏ YES ❏ NO

WHAT WILL WE KEEP IT IN?
A special box or basket ❏ YES ❏ NO
A trash can ❏ YES ❏ NO
OTHER
_____

WHO WILL TAKE IT OUT EVERY WEEK?

Recycling schedule:

WEEK ONE: *me*
WEEK TWO:
WEEK THREE:
WEEK FOUR:

CREATE A COMPOST PILE IN YOUR BACKYARD

Composting is the process of turning food scraps and yard trimmings (like grass and leaves) into soil. By setting up a compost pile, you can reduce the amount of waste that goes into landfills and improve the quality of the soil in your backyard. After getting your parents' permission, start a compost pile. Here's how:

1 FIND A SPOT. Pick an area in the yard that's about four feet by four feet. Keep it far from the house but near a water source (such as a hose) and in some shade.

2 CONTAIN IT. If your parents don't want a big pile of compost in their backyard, you can turn an old garbage bin into a compost bin. You'll need:

* An old plastic garbage bin
* A hammer and one big nail

Under adult supervision, using the hammer and nail, poke holes about four inches apart all over the garbage bin.

3 REGULATE. Put up a sign in your house telling your family what they can and cannot add to the pile.

DO COMPOST:

* VEGETABLES
* EGGSHELLS
* COFFEE GROUNDS AND FILTERS
* TEABAGS
* LEAVES
* GRASS
* YARD CLIPPINGS
* VACUUM CLEANER LINT
* WOOL AND COTTON RAGS
* SHREDDED NEWSPAPER

DON'T COMPOST:

* MEATS
* DAIRY FOODS (YOGURT, CHEESE, OTHER MILK PRODUCTS)
* ANY FATS, OIL, OR GREASE
* HARD OR TOUGH MATERIALS, SUCH AS CORN COBS, STALKS, AND COCONUTS

4 LAY THE FOUNDATION. Start your pile with a four-inch layer of leaves, soil, and yard trimmings. Some tips:

* Compost food scraps with an equal amount of yard trimmings and newspaper.
* Add clean cat litter to absorb smells if your compost starts to stink.
* In dry weather, add a small amount of water to the pile.

Environment

5 **MIX IT UP.** Oxygen helps to break down the waste, so turn the pile every few weeks with a rake or shovel.

> **GROSS-OUT ALERT!**
> Don't be freaked out if the pile gets hot and full of worms. The microbes that are breaking down the material generate heat; and worms love the nutrients! Their munching helps turn the waste into compost.

6 **PILE IT ON.** Continue to add to your compost pile. Keep a special bin in the kitchen for compost scraps and dump them on your pile every couple of days. (Tip: If you're worried about the smell, keep the scraps in a bag in the freezer.)

7 **BE PATIENT.** Compost is done in three to six months. When it's dark and crumbly, spread it under bushes or in the garden and watch those plants thrive!

NOTES:

CLEAN UP A SECTION OF YOUR TOWN

If you want to get serious about ridding your town of pollution and trash, it's time to get out there and get your hands dirty! Here's how to organize a cleanup:

1 | **PICK A PLACE.** What's the grossest spot in town? Is there a place where plastic garbage bags and soda cans seem to gather?

* Along a river, stream, or pond
* Park or town green

I'M GOING TO CLEAN UP:

_____
_____
_____

AFTER I'VE DONE THAT, I'LL CLEAN UP:

_____
_____
_____

2 **GET THE OKAY.** If it's just you and a couple of friends, you probably don't need official permission to pick up trash. But if you're going to get a huge crew together, then you'll need to run it by some people.

IS YOUR CLEANUP SITE ON PUBLIC PROPERTY? (If it is a park, or piece of green in town, the answer is probably yes.)

If it is, call up the Department of Recreation or Department of Public Works.

IS YOUR CLEANUP SITE ON PRIVATE PROPERTY? (If it's in an area with a lot of houses, or a field out in the country, the answer is probably yes.)

Talk to the landowner to get permission. You may have to knock on some doors. (Your Elevator Pitch from Project #24 on page 193 would be helpful here.)

3 **SET A DATE.** Pick a weekend day that works for you and your team. Make sure it doesn't overlap with sports practice or other activities. Keep in mind the following:

* Saturday mornings are usually the best time.

* You don't want the weather to be too hot or too cold (think early fall or spring).

* Pick a date that is at least eight weeks away to make sure you have enough time to plan and get volunteers on board.

* Schedule an alternate date, just in case it rains!

DATE AND TIME OF CLEANUP:

_____
_____

RAIN DATE AND TIME:

_____
_____

Environment

119

4 **VISIT THE SITE.** Grab a few of your team members and check out your cleanup location.

5 **DECIDE ON DISPOSAL.** If your cleanup goes well, you'll need help hauling away all the trash and junk you've collected. If it's a ton of stuff, you may need to call in professionals.

IS THERE A BATHROOM NEARBY?
❑ YES ❑ NO

If not, ask a nearby business owner if they will donate their bathroom for a few hours on the day of the cleanup.

IS IT EASY TO GET TO?
❑ YES ❑ NO

If not, choose a meeting place in the middle of town and drive or walk to the site together. (If you need to drive, make sure someone will be available to give you a ride before you do too much planning.)

CONTACT YOUR TOWN'S DEPARTMENT OF SANITATION TO SEE IF THEY CAN HELP YOU WITH:

Removal of trash bags ❑ YES ❑ NO

Removal of recyclables ❑ YES ❑ NO

Removal of big items from the site (like appliances or tires) ❑ YES ❑ NO

YOU CAN FIND THEIR NUMBER ONLINE OR IN THE YELLOW PAGES UNDER "SANITATION":

PHONE NUMBER:
_____

CONTACT NAME:
_____

6 **GET YOUR SUPPLIES.** There's a good chance that you can get local businesses (think hardware stores) to donate materials such as trash bags and rakes. Here are some things you'll probably need:

★ Heavy-duty trash bags

★ Different-colored bags or boxes for recyclable materials

★ Work gloves

★ Rakes

★ Shovels

★ Wheelbarrows

★ First-aid kit (Band-Aids, antibacterial gel)

★ Hand sanitizer

★ Water (you're going to get thirsty!)

★ A sign-in sheet to collect the

names and contact info of your volunteers.

7 **GET THE WORD OUT.** Post flyers at school, around town, at your place of worship, all over the place! (Check out Project #30 on page 216 for tips on how to make a great flyer.) Be sure to include:

* Date
* Time
* Location of the cleanup
* Where everyone will meet
* Rain date

8 **ROCK YOUR CLEANUP!** How did you do?

WE COLLECTED _____ BAGS OF LITTER.

9 **SAY THANKS.** You couldn't have done it on your own.

* Send thank-you notes to your volunteers.

* Send thank-yous to the people who gave you permission and any local businesses that donated goods to the event. (For great thank-you notes, see Project #39 on page 250.)

NOTES:
_____
_____
_____
_____
_____
_____
_____
_____
_____
_____
_____
_____
_____
_____
_____
_____
_____
_____
_____
_____
_____
_____
_____
_____
_____
_____
_____
_____
_____
_____
_____
_____
_____
_____
_____
_____
_____

Environment

ORGANIZE A JUMPING-JACK-ATHON

Exercise keeps you healthy, so what better way to raise awareness (and money) about a health issue than getting really sweaty? A jumping jack marathon to benefit the health organization of your choice is a fun way to raise awareness about the importance of exercise *and* raise money for a really good cause! Here's how it works:

| THE BASIC IDEA. You promise to do a certain number of jumping jacks (20, 40, 60, 100!), and get people to donate money if you reach that goal. For example, you could promise to do 100 jumping jacks for $20. The more kids who participate, the more pledges you'll get and the more money you'll raise.

HOW MUCH WOULD YOU LIKE PEOPLE TO PLEDGE?

For $1, I will do _____ jumping jacks

For $5, I will do _____ jumping jacks

For $10, I will do _____ jumping jacks

For $20, I will do _____ jumping jacks

You can also have kids raise money in teams so they can trade off with the jumping jacks. One hundred jumping jacks could get tiring!

HOW MANY TEAMS DO YOU NEED?

HOW MANY KIDS DID YOU WANT TO SIGN UP?

2 GET YOUR FRIENDS ON BOARD. You'll need a couple of people to count the jumping jacks, and you'll also need someone to collect donations. List their names and contact info here:

Helper #1's Name:

Contact Info:

Responsibilities:

Helper #2's Name:

Contact Info:

Responsibilities:

Helper #3's Name:

Contact Info:

Responsibilities:

If you need more room, flip to page 268.

Health & Fitness

3 **SELECT YOUR ORG.** What specific health issue do you want to support? Maybe asthma is an issue in your community, or maybe you have a family member with diabetes and you want to raise funds for that. Here are some organizations we like:

DIABETES

- •Change for the Children
  CHANGEFORTHECHILDREN.ORG
- •Juvenile Diabetes Research Foundation
  JDRF.ORG

ASTHMA

- •American Lung Association
  LUNGUSA.ORG
- •American Asthma Foundation
  AMERICANASTHMAFOUNDATION.ORG

HEART DISEASE

- •American Heart Association
  AMERICANHEART.ORG
- •World Heart Foundation
  WORLD-HEART.ORG

CANCER

- •American Cancer Association
  CANCER.ORG
- •Ronald McDonald House
  RMHC.ORG

GENERAL ORGANIZATION FOR SICK KIDS

- •Make a Wish Foundation
  WISH.ORG

I'M GOING TO RAISE MONEY FOR:

_____

_____

4 **PICK A PLACE.** Pick a spot that's easy to get to and is big enough for a bunch of kids jumping like crazy. Make sure it's a place that will welcome noise and activity. Here are some ideas to get you started:

❑ Local park

❑ School track

❑ Rec center

❑ Your backyard

❑ Other places:

_____

_____

_____

EVENT LOCATION:

_____

IF I CAN'T GO THERE, THEN I'LL TRY:

_____

5 **PICK A TIME.** When do you want to have the event? (Weekends work best!) Pick out a few days, just in case some of them conflict with other events around town or at school. And be sure to schedule a rain date in case it rains.

EVENT DATE:

_____

EVENT LENGTH: FROM _____ TO _____

Health & Fitness

123

6 **SPREAD THE WORD.** Advertise with fun posters and flyers (see Project #30 on page 216 for flyer tips). Make sure the flyers include:

★ When the event will take place
★ Where the event will take place

7 **GET PARTICIPANTS.** Make a donor sign-up sheet for your participants. It can look like this:

Participant (or Team) Name:

_____

Donor Sign-up

DONOR	AMOUNT DONATED	# OF JUMPING JACKS

8 **THE BIG DAY.** Before you kick off the jumping jacks, tell them where they can hand in their donations and thank them for their support. Don't forget to announce how much money you raised!

IT COULD SOUND SOMETHING LIKE THIS:

"Thanks to everyone for coming out today—especially to the jumpers who volunteered to get really sweaty and the generous donors who helped us raise an awesome [amount raised]! This money is going to [name of org] which is an important cause fighting to end [health issue]."

9 **DONATE THE MONEY!** Give the donations to a parent or teacher at school so they can write you a check. Check the website to find out who the checks should be made out to and where they should be sent.

MAKE CHECK PAYABLE TO:
_____

MAIL IT TO:
_____
_____

Health & Fitness

CREATE A PETITION FOR A HEALTHIER LUNCH

Tired of mashed potatoes and mystery meat for lunch every day? Ick! Get your entire grade to sign a petition asking your school to serve more fresh fruits and veggies. All those signatures will show your school's administration that the students want change. Here's how to get one going:

> "Vegetables and fruit are part of a healthy, well-balanced meal. We don't get enough fresh fruits and veggies at lunch. We're signing this petition to ask that the school give us more."

1 **GET IT DOWN ON PAPER.** Check out Project #32 on page 225 for a petition template. At the top, include facts about healthy eating.

FACT 1: Good nutrition and a balanced diet help kids grow up healthy.

FACT 2: Over the past 30 years, the number of overweight children has doubled and the number of overweight teenagers has tripled. This is due in large part to unhealthy eating habits.

FACT 3: A can of soda contains 10 teaspoons of sugar.

Then add a statement explaining **WHY** you're creating the petition, and **WHAT** exactly you want to happen. It can read something like this:

The signature page should have some columns to get necessary info: name, grade, and, of course, signature. Be sure you make enough copies! It should look something like this:

SIGNATURE	NAME	GRADE	DATE

TIP: Make photocopies of the signature page whenever you can so you have backup copies of your petition.

2 **GET HELP!** Recruit a team to help you collect signatures. Create a schedule with the dates, time, and locations where you and your volunteers will be collecting signatures.

Health & Fitness

125

Helper #1's Name: _____

Contact Info: _____

Location: _____

Helper #2's Name: _____

Contact Info: _____

Location: _____

Helper #3's Name: _____

Contact Info: _____

Location: _____

If you need more room, flip to page 268.

3 GET YOUR MATERIALS. Here's what you'll need:

- ★ Copies of the petition
- ★ Extra signature sheets
- ★ Pens
- ★ Clipboards

4 LOCATION, LOCATION, LOCATION. Find areas with high foot traffic—in the hallways before class, the basketball courts during recess, the cafeteria at lunchtime. Have your Elevator Pitch from Project #24 on page 193 ready to go before you start approaching your classmates.

5 ONLINE OR OFF-LINE? Nowadays you can do a petition on the Internet. If you have a lot of people's e-mail addresses you can give these sites a shot.

CHECK OUT:
- ★ GOPETITION.COM
- ★ PETITIONONLINE.COM
- ★ IPETITIONS.COM
- ★ PETITIONSPOT.COM

6 TURN IT IN. Once you've collected all your signatures, bring it to your principal. Tell him or her that your grade has spoken!

WHAT DID HE/SHE SAY?

_____
_____
_____

NOTES:

_____
_____
_____
_____
_____
_____
_____
_____
_____
_____
_____
_____
_____
_____

COLLECT FUN STUFF FOR SICK KIDS

Imagine having to spend days, weeks, or even months in a hospital, missing out on school and friends. Brighten a sick kid's day with a bag full of toys, books, and games. Hold a drive to collect the goodies and deliver them to a local children's hospital. Here's how:

1 CHOOSE A HOSPITAL. Each hospital has different donations rules so be sure to contact the hospital or medical center first.

HOSPITAL: _____

ADDRESS: _____

PHONE NUMBER: _____

If no nearby hospital is accepting donations, contact local churches, temples, or community centers and ask if they work with children's hospitals.

ORGANIZATION: _____

ADDRESS: _____
_____
_____

PHONE NUMBER: _____

2 MAKE A LIST. When you call them up, be ready with a few important questions:

WHAT WOULD YOU LIKE ME TO COLLECT?

❏ Board games

❏ Cards

❏ Books for young readers

❏ Books for older kids

❏ Video games

❏ DVDs

❏ Markers/crayons

❏ Construction paper

❏ Craft materials

❏ Play-Doh

❏ Puzzles

❏ Blocks

❏ Stuffed animals

❏ Action figures

WHAT CONDITION CAN THEY BE IN?
❏ New ❏ Gently used ❏ Both

HOW SHOULD I DELIVER DONATIONS?
❏ All together
❏ In individual "kits"

---

3 GET THE GO-AHEAD. Ask the principal if you can host a drive at school. (Be ready with your Elevator Pitch from Project #24 on page 193.)

4 SET THE DATES. Decide how long your drive will run. A week is

Health & Fitness

good. Two weeks is even better! Any longer than that, and people might start to lose interest.

THE DRIVE WILL RUN
FROM _____ **TO** _____

5 GET YOUR TEACHERS ON BOARD. Ask your teachers if they'll agree to do something crazy if you reach a certain goal, like promise to wear a ridiculous T-shirt to work or shave their head.

6 GET YOUR FRIENDS ON BOARD. It's more fun when you're doing it with your buds.

Helper #1's Name:
Contact Info:
Responsibilities:

Helper #2's Name:
Contact Info:
Responsibilities:

Helper #3's Name:
Contact Info:
Responsibilities:

7 GET YOUR BOXES. Have everyone search their homes for large cardboard boxes. Also ask the principal's office or your teachers if they have boxes to spare. Decorate the boxes so they pop!

8 SPREAD THE WORD. Make posters and flyers ahead of time giving people the details. The more people know about it, the more donations you'll get. (See Project #30 on page 216 for great poster- and flyer-making tips.) Make sure the poster has the following:

* The days of the drive

* Where the student should drop off the goodies

* What kind of stuff you're collecting

* What kind of stuff you're NOT collecting

* If the items must be new, be sure to say so

9 USE YOUR LUNGS. Ask if you can get up during morning announcements or homeroom. Or use your big mouth during lunch or between periods and shout out the cause.

"Listen up! Every day thousands of kids across the U.S. are stuck in hospitals. They're poked and prodded, and they miss out on Mom's cooking, going to school and parties, and just living life. We're helping out by hosting a collection drive on [days of drive]. Just drop off [items you need] in the boxes found in [location #1] and [location #2]. Let's show these kids we care!"

10 **SHOW OFF THE GOODS.** Set a goal and update the sign every day with the amount of donations collected and the amount still to go.

★ Ask if you can put the poster in the school office or in a place where everyone passes like the lunchroom or by the main doors.

★ Have teachers write the goal on their chalkboards.

MY GOAL:

_____

11 **CLOSE DOWN.** Officially end the drive by placing the poster with the final amount of donations collected.

12 **ASSEMBLE THE KITS.** If you're making individual kits, make sure you distribute the goodies evenly (don't give one kid three packs of cards and zero books). Add a little note of encouragement or maybe some artwork to help bring a smile to their face.

13 **CONTACT THE HOSPITAL.** Tell them you have donations to drop off and set up a time to hand them over. Make sure you have a ride if you need one!

DROP-OFF DAY:

_____

WHO'S GOING TO TAKE ME?:

_____

Health & Fitness

ORGANIZE A WATERMELON-EATING CONTEST

The simplest way to help a local food bank or soup kitchen is by sending money. Your allowance probably won't cut it, so why not throw a fund-raiser? Organize a watermelon-eating contest to raise money for a local food bank. Here's how:

| THE BASIC IDEA. In a watermelon-eating contest, people race to eat as many slices of watermelon in a certain amount of time (say 10 minutes). It's sloppy, loud, and can get pretty hilarious! Ask each person to donate $5 to participate and you'll see those dollar signs add up.

2 CHOOSE A FOOD BANK. Each organization has different rules on donating money so contact a food bank first.

★ Check the yellow pages. Look up "food bank" or "food pantry" or "soup kitchen."

★ Or, go online to Feeding America and type in your state and zip code:

FEEDINGAMERICA.ORG/FOODBANK-RESULTS.ASPX

ADDRESS:

PHONE NUMBER:

COMMUNITY THEY SERVE:

3 PICK A PLACE. Find a location for the contest that's easy to get to. It'll be messy and noisy so have it outside! Some places to try:

❑ Local park

❑ School track

❑ Rec center

❑ Your backyard

❑ Other places:

EVENT LOCATION:

4 PICK A TIME. When do you want to have the event? (Weekends work best!) Pick out a few days, just in case some of them conflict with other events going on around town or at school. Make sure the weather's nice—no one wants to eat watermelon in the cold!

EVENT DATE:

5 GET YOUR WATERMELONS. Go around to local supermarkets and ask to speak to the manager. Tell them about the competition and ask if they'll donate watermelons to help support your cause. (Be sure to have your Elevator Pitch from Project #24 on page 193 ready to go!) You

Homelessness & Hunger

may have to go to more than one store. Don't get discouraged!

> Store #1:
> Spoke to:
> Number of watermelons
> they will donate:
>
> Store #2:
> Spoke to:
> Number of watermelons
> they will donate:
>
> Store #3:
> Spoke to:
> Number of watermelons
> they will donate:

If they don't have watermelons to spare, ask if they'll donate a prize for the winner.

THE PRIZE WILL BE:

6 **ADVERTISE.** Spread the word with fun posters and flyers (see Project #30 on page 216 for flyer tips.) Make sure the flyers include:

* ★ Event date
* ★ Event location
* ★ Event time
* ★ What people should wear (it's going to get messy!)

7 **THE BIG DAY.** Before you kick off the event, introduce yourself, talk about the goal of the contest and why this cause is so important to you.

DON'T FORGET TO ANNOUNCE HOW MUCH MONEY YOU RAISED!

WE RAISED:

8 **AND THE WINNER IS...** Present the winner with their prize.

9 **DONATE THE MONEY!** Pick someone really responsible to collect the donations from the participants. Give the donations to a grown-up so they can write you a check. Be sure to find out from the food bank who the checks should be made out to and where they should be sent.

MAKE CHECK PAYABLE TO:

MAIL IT TO:

10 **SAY THANKS.** Write thank-you notes to all the stores who donated watermelons. For tips on writing a great thank you, see Project #39 on page 250.

HOLD A CLOTHING DRIVE

Imagine not having a home of your own or enough money to buy yourself clothes. Help those in need by organizing a drive to collect gently used clothing for a local homeless shelter. Here's how:

1 CHOOSE A SHELTER. Contact a local shelter with a drop-off location near you to find out what clothing they'll accept.

> ★ Check the yellow pages. Look up "homeless shelter" or "homeless services"
>
> ★ Or go online and try the Homeless Shelter Director at: **HOMELESSSHELTERDIRECTORY.ORG**

If there's no organization near you, you can ask at local:

> ★ Churches
> ★ Temples
> ★ Community centers

WHERE DID YOU DECIDE?

ORGANIZATION:

ADDRESS:

PHONE NUMBER:

2 WHAT DO THEY NEED? Once you have a shelter or organization in mind, call them up and ask to speak to the person who handles donations.

CONTACT NAME:

PHONE NUMBER:

HERE'S WHAT YOU NEED TO ASK THEM:

What kind of clothes do they need most?

> ★ Coats (check one)
> ❑ KIDS ❑ MEN ❑ WOMEN ❑ EVERYONE
>
> ★ Sweaters
> ❑ KIDS ❑ MEN ❑ WOMEN ❑ EVERYONE
>
> ★ Shirts
> ❑ KIDS ❑ MEN ❑ WOMEN ❑ EVERYONE
>
> ★ Pants
> ❑ KIDS ❑ MEN ❑ WOMEN ❑ EVERYONE
>
> ★ Shoes
> ❑ KIDS ❑ MEN ❑ WOMEN ❑ EVERYONE
>
> ★ Other:

Will they pick them up or will I have to drop them off?

They will pick up
❑ YES ❑ NO

I'll have to drop them off
❑ YES ❑ NO

3 GET THE GO-AHEAD. Ask the principal if you can host a clothing drive for homeless people. (Have your Elevator Pitch ready from Project #24 on page 193.)

Homelessness & Hunger

Have the following details available:

WHO YOU ARE COLLECTING FOR:

WHY:

WHEN YOU PLAN ON HAVING THE COLLECTION DRIVE:

OTHER:

☐ THE PRINCIPAL SAID YES
☐ THE PRINCIPAL SAID NO. THE REASONS HE/SHE GAVE:

If he or she said no, don't be discouraged. Maybe you can do this at your place of worship or local community center.

4 **GET YOUR TEACHERS ON BOARD.** Ask your teacher if they'll do something crazy if you reach a certain goal, like promise to wear a ridiculous T-shirt to work or shave their heads.

MY TEACHERS ARE GOING TO HELP BY:

5 **GET YOUR FRIENDS ON BOARD.** Who's going to help? List their names and contact info here:

Helper #1's Name:
Contact Info:
Responsibilities:

Helper #2's Name:
Contact Info:
Responsibilities:

Helper #3's Name:
Contact Info:
Responsibilities:

6 **SET THE DATES.** Decide how long your drive will run. A week is good. Two weeks is even better! Any longer then that, and people might start to lose interest.

THE DRIVE WILL RUN FROM
TO

7 **LOCATION, LOCATION, LOCATION.** Figure out where you want to place the collection bins. Places with heavy foot traffic work the best.

I'M GOING TO PUT BINS IN THE FOLLOWING PLACES:

❑ School entrances and exits

❑ In the cafeteria

❑ Outside the auditorium

❑ Other places:

_____

_____

_____

_____

8 **GET YOUR BOXES.** Have everyone search their homes for large cardboard boxes. Ask the principal's office or your teachers if they have boxes to spare. Decorate the boxes so they pop!

9 **SPREAD THE WORD.** Make posters and flyers with all of the details. The more people who know about the drive, the more donations you'll get. Make sure the poster has the following:

★ The days of the drive

★ Where the students should drop off the clothes

★ List the items that your organization says it needs

★ Emphasize that the items don't have to be new but should be gently used—that means no holes or stains!

10 **USE YOUR LUNGS.** Ask if you can make an announcement during morning announcements or homeroom. Or use your big mouth during lunch or in between periods and shout out the cause.

"Listen up! Thousands of people across the U.S. are homeless. In fact, 1 in 3 homeless people in the U.S. are under the age of 18. We're helping out by hosting a clothing drive on (days of drive). Just drop off clothes (what do you need?) in (collection box locations). Let's show people we care!"

SHOW OFF THE GOODS. Display the amount of donations you've collected on huge poster boards. Update the sign every day with the amount collected, and the amount still to go.

* Ask the school if you can put the poster in the front office or a place where everyone passes

* Update teachers who are writing it on their chalkboards

12 CLOSE DOWN. Officially end the drive by placing your final poster with the amount of donations you collected in the main lobby or lunchroom.

13 DONATE! Call up the shelter or organization and let them know you're ready to drop off the clothes or have them come pick them up. Schedule a time and a day. Make sure you have a ride if you need one!

DROP-OFF/PICK-UP DAY:

WHO WILL DRIVE ME?

HOST A HUNGER BANQUET

Over nine million people, including five million children, die worldwide each year because of hunger and malnutrition. A simple hunger banquet can make your classmates more aware of how others in the world—and maybe in your community—face the daily problem of hunger. Here's how to host one:

1 MAKE YOUR CASE. You'll have to get permission from your teacher or principal. Explain what you're doing and why and give a quick description of how you're going to do it. (Have your Elevator Pitch from Project #24 on page 193 handy.)

It could sound something like this.

WHAT YOU'RE DOING:

" I'd like to use snack time to explain how big a problem hunger is around the world."

WHY YOU'RE DOING IT:

" Most people don't know that 15 percent of the world consumes more food than they require while 50 percent of the world does not get enough food."

HOW YOU'RE DOING IT:

" I plan on helping my classmates understand this problem with an exercise that will show them how unfair it is."

2 GET SOME SNACKS. See if the lunchroom will donate additional snacks for the day so you have enough to help your class really get the point. It doesn't have to be fancy—just make sure you have enough—an apple, orange, cookie—for each kid in the class.

NUMBER OF SNACKS:

_____

WHAT WILL THOSE SNACKS BE?

_____
_____
_____
_____
_____

WHO WILL DONATE THEM?

_____
_____
_____
_____
_____

3 PRESENTATION TIME. Begin with a short explanation of the world hunger problem. Here's an example of what you can say:

> "Half the world—nearly three billion people—lives on less than $2 a day. And 15 percent—that's 900 million—eat more than they need to, 35 percent (210 million) have just enough to eat, while 50 percent (three billion) don't get enough food every day. Those numbers may be a lot for you to understand, so we're going to do an exercise that will help put this into simple terms."

4 DIVIDE THEM UP. Split your class into three groups: a group that makes up 15 percent of the class; a group that makes up 35 percent of the class; and a group that makes up 50 percent of the class. So if there are 30 students in your class, the groups should be made up like this:

- **5 STUDENTS IN GROUP A (THAT'S THE 15 PERCENT)**

- **10 STUDENTS IN GROUP B (THAT'S THE 35 PERCENT)**

- **15 STUDENTS IN GROUP C (THAT'S THE 50 PERCENT)**

5 DISTRIBUTE. Hand out food to the different groups.

- ★ Give Group A two snacks each and tell them to enjoy

- ★ Give Group B one snack each

- ★ Give Group C one quarter of a snack

6 TALK IT OUT. Discuss the following questions:

- ★ How do you feel that five of your classmates got two snacks? Is this fair?

- ★ How do you think this affects people's health?

NOTES:

Homelessness & Hunger

WRITE AN AMNESTY INTERNATIONAL LETTER

Amnesty International fights to free political prisoners—people who are put in jail for speaking their mind or for speaking out against their government. Amnesty International uses letter-writing campaigns asking government officials to free political prisoners and to protect them from abuse, neglect, and torture while in prison. Here's how to add your own letter to the pile:

1 DO YOUR RESEARCH. Head to Amnesty International's website to browse through stories of people who need your help now.

★ Visit: **AMNESTYUSA.ORG**

★ Or just type "AI Kids" into a Web browser like Google or Yahoo.

2 PICK A PERSON. Browse through the stories of people all over the world whose rights are being denied. Or, take a look at the "AI Kids" Urgent Action for the month.

3 FOLLOW DIRECTIONS. Each case is different. Be sure to read all the details about the prisoner you are writing about. Amnesty International will include the address and give you the main points of the person's case.

4 GET WRITING. Start by writing the official's complete address at the top. Also include your address so the official can respond if needed. (Check out the sample letter on the opposite page.)

5 USE THE PROPER TITLE. Titles can range from Mr. and Mrs., or something fancy like Her Majesty. Amnesty International will let you know how to address the person you are writing to, so follow their lead.

6 BE DEMANDING. Start the letter by laying out the big picture:

WHAT'S YOUR MAIN CONCERN?

_____
_____
_____

WHAT DO YOU WANT THE GOVERNMENT TO DO ABOUT IT?

_____
_____
_____

7 SHOW YOU KNOW YOUR STUFF. Write two or three sentences about the prisoner's story:

WHY IS THAT PERSON IN JAIL?

_____
_____
_____

HOW LONG HAVE THEY BEEN IN JAIL?

_____
_____
_____

8 KEEP AT IT. Visit Amnesty International every month to see if you prisoner has been freed. Unfortunately, it can take a lot of time and a lot of letters and international pressure to get a prisoner released from jail. You may want to resend your letter every 2–3 months.

Make your letter short, be polite, use the victim's name throughout the letter, and keep it simple and to the point!

February 25, 2010

Monsieur Akila Esso Boko
Ministre de l'Interieur et de la Securité
Rue Albert Sarraut
Lome, Togo

Dear Minister Boko:

I am concerned about reports that Marc Palanga was arrested on February 22 and may be at risk of torture. Please act immediately to protect Mr. Palanga from ill treatment while in detention at the Kara Police Station in northern Togo.

Marc Palanga, a local leader of the Union des forces du changement (UFC), has not used violence to express his views and yet he has been arrested several times for his peaceful involvement with this group. I have heard that many other people have also been treated badly or put in jail for speaking their minds. Please, I urge you to stop arresting Togo citizens, including Marc Palanga, and give them the opportunity to express themselves.

I would like to visit your beautiful country someday and hope to do so when the human rights of all citizens in Togo are respected. Thank you for looking into this matter and quickly releasing community activist Marc Palanga. Please let me know when you have allowed Marc Palanga his freedom.

Sincerely,
Stephanie Moore

Stephanie Moore
123 Activist Avenue
Nederland, CO 80466
USA

ORGANIZE A DAY OF SILENCE

People living in the United States and many other democratic countries have the right to freedom of speech, but every day, people around the world risk violence or arrest for speaking out. It's easy to forget how lucky we are to be able to speak our minds. Raise awareness about those people who *don't* have freedom of speech by holding a Day of Silence at school. Here's how:

1 GET THE OKAY. Some teachers consider a Day of Silence to be disruptive, so make sure to clear it with the school administration first. Have your Elevator Pitch from Project #24 on page 193 ready.

☐ THE PRINCIPAL SAID YES

☐ THE PRINCIPAL SAID NO. THE REASONS HE/SHE GAVE:

_____

_____

_____

DON'T TAKE NO FOR AN ANSWER! If you can't get permission for a whole day, try to convince them to let you do it for an hour, or even have a moment of silence at homeroom or during lunch.

2 PICK YOUR CAUSE. It's best to have a specific cause that you're protesting—a person or group that was recently silenced.

HERE ARE A FEW EXAMPLES:

★ *In 2009, Iranian men and women took to the streets when they thought that their votes weren't being counted. Even though their protests were peaceful, they were beaten and arrested.*

★ *Journalists in Cambodia can be put in jail for writing negative articles about their government.*

★ *Members of the Moroccan Association for Human Rights were arrested by police after participating in peaceful demonstrations and using slogans that criticized the country's king.*

The international section of the newspaper is a great place to find more stories like these. You can also check in with organizations that make it their business to keep track of human rights violations around the world:

★ *Amnesty International:* **AMNESTYUSA.ORG**

★ *Human Rights Watch:* **HRW.ORG**

3 PICK A DAY. Schedule your day of silence. Again, don't forget to run the date by your school officials.

THE DAY OF SILENCE WILL BE ON:

_____

4 SPREAD THE WORD. You may need to do a lot of convincing to get your friends to be totally quiet for a whole day. Hand out flyers, put up posters, and just generally chat it up. See Project #30 on page 216 for tips on making eye-catching flyers and posters.

5 CIRCULATE A SIGN-UP SHEET. Pass a few clipboards around classrooms to get people to sign up for the day.

6 SILENCE CARDS. Make cards that participants can give their teachers and other kids to explain why they're not talking. Here's a good example:

> To my teacher: Today I will not be able to actively participate in class because I am participating in the Day of Silence to honor those people who do not have free speech around the world. I hope to spread the word about these people and to learn about their struggle today. I hope you'll join me in working to protect their human rights and freedom of speech.

7 ZIP YOUR LIP! After you've let people know that you'll be participating, wake up on the Day of Silence and zip it up! Honor those you are fighting for by trying to remain as quiet as possible throughout the day.

8 REFLECT ON YOUR DAY. At the end of the day, invite people to join you for snacks and a gab-fest. Some questions to ask:

WHAT DID YOU LEARN?

WHAT WAS HARD?

WHAT WAS EASIER THAN YOU THOUGHT IT WOULD BE?

WHAT OTHER THINGS CAN WE DO TO PROTECT FREE SPEECH?

DO A POSTER CAMPAIGN FOR HUMAN RIGHTS

The United Nations' Universal Declaration of Human Rights outlines the rights that belong to all people. Educate people about this big document with a poster campaign. If you don't know what your rights are, how can you protect them? Here's how to get started:

I **GET THE OKAY.** Decide where you'd like to hang your posters. If you want to post your signs around school (we recommend it!), check with your administrator or principal to make sure you are allowed. Explain why you think it's important to educate your classmates on human rights. (Be ready with your Elevator Pitch from Project #24 on page 193.)

☐ THE PRINCIPAL SAID YES

☐ THE PRINCIPAL SAID NO. THE REASONS HE/SHE GAVE:

_____

_____

_____

_____

2 **DO YOUR RESEARCH.** The actual Declaration of Human Rights is long and has a lot of fancy words in it. The good news is that the United Nations has a simpler version that you can find online. Get on the Internet and type in this exact address:

WWW.UN.ORG/CYBERSCHOOLBUS/ HUMANRIGHTS/RESOURCES/PLAIN.ASP

THE DECLARATION HAS 30 ARTICLES. HERE ARE THE FIRST FIVE:

1. When children are born, they are free and each should be treated in the same way. They have reason and conscience and should act towards one another in a friendly manner.

2. Everyone can claim the following rights, despite

★ being a different gender

★ having a different skin color

★ speaking a different language

★ thinking different things

★ believing in another religion

★ owning more or less

★ being born in another social group

★ coming from another country

3. You have the right to live, and to live in freedom and safety.

4. Nobody has the right to treat you as his or her slave, and you should not make anyone your slave.

5. Nobody has the right to torture you.

3 **DESIGN YOUR POSTERS.** Pick 10 of your favorite lines and write each on its own poster. Jazz them up with pictures and bright colors so they really pop!

Write your 10 favorite lines here!

1. _____
2. _____
3. _____
4. _____
5. _____
6. _____
7. _____
8. _____
9. _____
10. _____

Do all 30, if you want!

4 **SPREAD THE WORD.** Hang your posters as far as the eye can see! Make sure they're posted in areas of your school that have heavy foot traffic. The more eyes on them, the better!

NOTES:
_____
_____
_____
_____
_____
_____
_____
_____
_____
_____

LIST WHERE YOU PLAN TO HANG EACH POSTER:

POSTER #1: _____
POSTER #2: _____
POSTER #3: _____
POSTER #4: _____
POSTER #5: _____
POSTER #6: _____
POSTER #7: _____
POSTER #8: _____
POSTER #9: _____
POSTER #10: _____

__ _Poverty_

HOLD A PENNY WAR

Are there rivalries between the grades at your school? Use that competitive streak for good and hold a "Penny War" and raise money to donate to an antipoverty organization. See if your grade can win! Here's how:

1 WHAT IS IT? A Penny War is a fun way to fund-raise. Each grade has a big jar with their name on it. People drop money into the jar, but there's a twist:

* Pennies count as one point, but other coins and cash count as negative amounts. So, if you want the other grades to lose, put pennies in your jar and nickels, dimes, quarters, and dollar bills into their jar.

* At the end of the day, each grade's points are counted and written down.

* When the competition ends, the grade with the fewest points wins!

2 WHO WILL YOU SUPPORT? Choose which antipoverty organization to support.

HERE ARE TWO OF OUR FAVORITES:

* Feeding America (feedingamerica .org) battles hunger in the U.S. The organization helps 37 million people and gives 2.5 billion pounds of food to soup kitchens, shelters, and after-school programs.

* UNICEF (unicefusa.org) works in 150 countries to save the lives of children in poverty. They assist with health care, nutrition, and clean water.

3 GET THE OKAY. Ask your teacher or principal if you can hold a Penny War to raise money for your organization.

❑ **THE PRINCIPAL SAID YES**
❑ **THE PRINCIPAL SAID NO. THE REASONS HE/SHE GAVE:**

_____
_____

4 GET THE SUPPLIES. You'll need:

❑ A table in the lunchroom or other busy area for the times you are collecting money

❑ An empty jar for each grade (these need to stay in a safe place like the front office or a classroom)

5 PICK A PRIZE. The winning grade could get:

* 10 more minutes at lunch for a week

* Candy donated by your school or teachers

* Front row seats to the best assembly of the year

* Other ideas:

_____
_____

144

6 PICK THE POINTS. Decide how many points each coin or dollar bill is worth.

FOR EXAMPLE:

Penny   = 1 point
Nickel   = 5 points
Dime   = 10 points
Quarter   = 25 points
Dollar   = 100 points

7 SCHEDULE IT. Arrange with the school administration what times you can collect the money for the Penny War.

BEFORE SCHOOL

From _____ until _____

DURING LUNCH

From _____ until _____

AFTER SCHOOL

From _____ until _____

8 GET VOLUNTEERS. You don't want to run the table all by yourself. Get friends to sign up for shifts.

Sign-Up Sheet

	NAME
DAY 1 Before School	
During Lunch	
After School	
DAY 2 Before School	
During Lunch	
After School	
DAY 3 Before School	
During Lunch	
After School	
DAY 4 Before School	
During Lunch	
After School	
DAY 5 Before School	
During Lunch	
After School	

Poverty

9 **USE YOUR LUNGS.** Promote the Penny War during morning announcements or just stand up during lunch and get everyone's attention. It could sound something like this:

"Listen up, everyone! Each grade is raising money to help fight poverty. Drop your pennies, nickels, dimes, and quarters in the jars. Here's the catch: Each coin is worth a certain number of points. You want to have the *least* number of points, so sabotage the other grades by stuffing their jars full of quarters and dimes! All of the money goes to [name of organization]. The collection table is located [location of table] and we will be collecting money [times of collection each day] from [first day of the Penny War] until [last day of the Penny War]. Good luck, and may the best grade win!"

10 **TALLY IT UP.** At the end of each time slot, give yourself 10 minutes to count each grade's earnings for the day. Example:

DAY 1

GRADE _____

COLLECTED:

_____ PENNIES × 1 POINTS= _____

_____ NICKELS × 5 POINTS= _____

_____ DIMES × 10 POINTS= _____

_____ QUARTERS × 25 POINTS= _____

_____ DOLLARS × 100 POINTS= _____

TOTAL POINTS= _____

DAY 2

GRADE _____

COLLECTED:

_____ PENNIES × 1 POINTS= _____

_____ NICKELS × 5 POINTS= _____

_____ DIMES × 10 POINTS= _____

_____ QUARTERS × 25 POINTS= _____

_____ DOLLARS × 100 POINTS= _____

TOTAL POINTS= _____

DAY 3

GRADE _____

COLLECTED:

_____ PENNIES × 1 POINTS= _____

_____ NICKELS × 5 POINTS= _____

_____ DIMES × 10 POINTS= _____

_____ QUARTERS × 25 POINTS= _____

_____ DOLLARS × 100 POINTS= _____

TOTAL POINTS= _____

DAY 4

GRADE _____

COLLECTED:

_____ PENNIES × I POINTS= _____

_____ NICKELS × 5 POINTS= _____

_____ DIMES × IO POINTS= _____

_____ QUARTERS × 25 POINTS= _____

_____ DOLLARS × IOO POINTS= _____

TOTAL POINTS= _____

DAY 5

GRADE _____

COLLECTED:

_____ PENNIES × I POINTS= _____

_____ NICKELS × 5 POINTS= _____

_____ DIMES × IO POINTS= _____

_____ QUARTERS × 25 POINTS= _____

_____ DOLLARS × IOO POINTS= _____

TOTAL POINTS= _____

Put the day's money in a safe place with a lock until the Penny War table opens the next day.

11 KEEP EVERYONE INTERESTED. Every day update everyone on the score:

"The Penny War is still going on! Everyone is doing a great job raising money to fight poverty. [grade] is in third place, [grade] is in second, and [grade]

is in the lead! If this is bad news for you, then keep those coins coming in! The Penny War will go on until [last day]. May the best grade win!"

12 WHO WON? After the last day, tally up the points and the cash. Who has the fewest points? Double-check your totals!

THE WINNER IS:

_____

HOW MUCH DID YOU RAISE?

_____

13 LET EVERYONE KNOW! Time for another announcement.

"Hey, everyone, the Penny War is now finished! Together, our school raised [total]. All of this money will to go [organization] to help fight poverty. While [third-place grade] came in third place, and [second-place grade] came in second, no one could beat the winners—the [winning grade]! Way to go! [announce what they won.]"

Poverty

14 DONATE YOUR MONEY. Here's the fun part—sending the money to the people who need it! You can't just mail a bunch of coins to the organization. You have a couple of options:

Option #1: Coinstar is a cool machine that will take your coins, count them, and automatically donate the money to charity. But first you need to make sure your charity is on their list.

① Visit **LOCATOR.COINSTAR.COM.**

② Type in your home address and scan the list of charities. (Feeding America and UNICEF are both on the list.) If your charity isn't on the list, jump down to Option #2.

③ Get an adult to drive you to the Coinstar location.

④ At the machine, follow the instructions and indicate that you want to donate the money.

⑤ Keep your receipt.

Option #2: Give the money to a parent or the school and have them write you a check. Contact the organization or visit their website to find out:

WHO THE CHECK SHOULD BE MADE OUT TO:

WHERE THE CHECK SHOULD BE MAILED TO:

If you are donating to either Feeding America or UNICEF, here's where to send it:

Make checks payable to "Feeding America" and mail to:

Feeding America
P.O. Box 96749
Washington, DC
20090-6749

Make checks payable to "U.S. Fund for UNICEF" and mail it to:

United States Fund for UNICEF
125 Maiden Lane
New York, NY 10038

NOTES:

HOLD A COAT DRIVE

Twenty percent of children in America live in poverty. That means that their parents can't afford to get them the basics—like clothes, school supplies, toiletries —even a winter coat. Get the students in your school to make a difference by holding a coat drive. (If you live in a warm area, you can hold a toy drive instead—see how on pages 94–97.)

| GET THE FACTS. First, you want to figure out how big a problem poverty is in your state. Go to the library and ask to see the census report from the previous year. Or, you can hop online and look it up yourself: **CENSUS.GOV/DID/WWW/SAIPE/COUNTY.HTML**

* Select your state and the most current year.
* Check the box asking how many people under 18 live in poverty in your state.
* Look at the column titled "number." That's the number of children living in poverty in your state.
* Write it down here: _____ children live in poverty in [your state].

2 GET THE GO-AHEAD. Ask your principal if you can host a drive to collect coats for those living in poverty.

❏ THE PRINCIPAL SAID YES
❏ THE PRINCIPAL SAID NO. THE REASONS HE/SHE GAVE:

_____
_____
_____

If your principal said no, you can do this at your place of worship or local community center.

3 FIND A PLACE TO DONATE. Contact the collection agency in your area.

|. Go to: ONEWARMCOAT.ORG/ORGANIZE.PHP
2. Click "Find an agency."
3. Enter your school's zip code.
4. Ask your parents how far they'd be willing to drive to help you drop off the coats, and enter in what they say. Five to 20 miles should do it.

What did you decide? →

Poverty

149

I'm going to donate the coats to:

ORGANIZATION NAME:

CONTACT NAME:

PHONE NUMBER:

If that doesn't work, I'm going to try:

ORGANIZATION NAME:

CONTACT NAME:

PHONE NUMBER:

4 **GET THE DETAILS.** Call the agency in your area and get some answers.

How would they like the coats delivered?

Folded in a box	❏ YES	❏ NO
Stuffed in a bag	❏ YES	❏ NO
Sorted by size	❏ YES	❏ NO

A different way:

Will they pick them up or will you have to drop them off?

They will pick up donations ❏ YES ❏ NO

If the answer is yes, when can they do a pick up?

THEY'LL PICK UP DONATIONS ON THESE DAYS:

AT THESE TIMES:

IF THE ANSWER IS NO, FIND OUT WHEN THEY ARE OPEN FOR DROP-OFFS.

THEY'LL ACCEPT DONATIONS ON THESE DAYS:

AT THESE TIMES:

Can the coats be gently used?
❏ YES ❏ NO

5 **GET YOUR TEACHERS ON BOARD.** Ask your teachers if they'll do something crazy if you reach a certain goal, like promise to wear a ridiculous T-shirt to work or shave their head. Make sure they write the goal on their chalkboard.

My teachers are going to help by:

6 GET YOUR FRIENDS ON BOARD. You don't want to do this alone. Who's going to help? List their names and contact info here:

Helper #1's Name:

Contact Info:

Responsibilities:

Helper #2's Name:

Contact Info:

Responsibilities:

Helper #3's Name:

Contact Info:

Responsibilities:

Need more room? Flip to page 268.

7 SET THE DATES. Decide how long your drive will run. A week is good. Two weeks is even better! Any longer than that, and people might start to lose interest.

THE DRIVE WILL RUN FROM _____ TO _____ .

8 LOCATION, LOCATION, LOCATION. Figure out where you want to place the collection bins. Places with heavy foot traffic work the best.

I'M GOING TO PUT BINS IN THE FOLLOWING PLACES:

❑ School entrances and exits

❑ In the cafeteria

❑ Outside the auditorium

❑ Other places:

_____

_____

9 SPREAD THE WORD. Make posters and flyers ahead of time giving people the details. The more people know about it, the more donations you'll get. Make sure the poster has the following:

★ Number of kids living in poverty in your state

★ Days of the drive

★ Donation box locations

10 USE YOUR LUNGS. Ask the front desk if you can speak about the drive during morning announcements or homeroom. Or use your big mouth during lunch or between periods and shout out the cause:

Poverty

"Listen up! One out of five American children lives in poverty and can't afford a lot basics, and that includes winter coats! We're helping out by hosting a coat drive on [days of drive]. Just drop off your new or gently used coats in the boxes found in [locations]. Let's help keep kids warm this winter!"

12 CLOSE DOWN. Officially end the drive by placing your final poster with the number of donations you collected in the main lobby or lunchroom. Write a special thanks to everyone who chipped in! (See project #39 on page 250 for some great ways to say thank you.)

HOW MANY COATS DID YOU COLLECT?

13 DROP-OFF/PICK-UP: Call the organization and tell them you're ready to make a donation.

11 SHOW OFF THE GOODS. Display the number of coats you collected on huge poster boards. You can update the sign every day with the number collected and the number still to go.

★ Ask if you can put the poster in the front office or a place where everyone passes by.

★ Update teachers who are writing the goal on their chalkboards.

MY GOAL IS TO COLLECT _____ COATS.

MAKE "STAND UP TO BULLIES" CARDS

Standing up to a bully can be tough, so why not get some practice? Ask your teacher if you can borrow class time one day to do an activity with the "Stand Up to Bullies" cards. Here are the details:

1 DIVIDE THE CLASS. Half the class will be bullies and half will be asked to use their Stand Up cards to figure out how to make a bully back down.

2 MAKE BULLY CARDS. Make at least five Bully cards. Each card should have a different kind of bullying or teasing. For example:

- ★ Teasing someone on the bus
- ★ Taking someone's food in the cafeteria
- ★ Gossiping about someone's clothes
- ★ Excluding someone from a game at recess
- ★ Writing or messaging mean comments online
- ★ Other ideas:

_____

_____

_____

3 MAKE STAND UP CARDS. These cards should say things like:

- ★ Don't react. Walk away.
- ★ Don't cry. Ignore the bully.
- ★ Smile or laugh. If you do the opposite of what the bully expects, it takes the fun away from bullying.
- ★ Communicate. Tell them how you feel. If you're calm, the bully loses power.
- ★ Tell an adult. If you need help, don't be afraid to ask. It's not tattling, it's standing up for yourself.
- ★ Other ideas:

_____

_____

_____

4 DISTRIBUTE THEM. Once your cards are made, pass them out to the class or ask your teacher to pass them out. Half should have Bully cards, the other half should have Stand Up cards.

5 ACT LIKE A BULLY. Have a student with a Bully card read or act out the scene.

6 NOW STAND UP! Ask the students with the Stand Up cards to respond by acting out how their Stand Up action will help get rid of the bully.

7 REFLECT IT. At the end of class, check in with your classmates to see what they learned. Ask them to write down any other suggestions for standing up to bullies on their own Stand Up cards.

8 SPREAD THE WORD. Hand the cards out to other classes or younger kids to help them stand up to bullies.

NOTES:

HOLD A "DON'T BE A STATISTIC" DAY

Did you know that every day about 75 American children are shot? Most recover—but about 15 out of the 75 don't survive! Scary stuff, right? How do you get people to see that this statistic is more than just a number? Here's a way to leave a lasting impression they can see and feel. Sometimes you really do have to see it to believe it!

1 **IDEA FACTORY.** The point of this demonstration is to use the school community itself to represent a statistic about the gun violence. How? Here are some ideas:

* **IDEA #1** Persuade 75 students to wear a special shirt, with the words "I'm one in 75" on the front. Have 15 of them have an additional statement on the back: "I didn't make it" or "I didn't recover." Now the community can really see the issue as they pass through the halls or while they eat lunch.

* **IDEA #2** Cover 75 random lockers with red construction paper. Add 75 more each day for a week. Make it dramatic, because the more attention you get, the larger the impact!

(Just be sure to get permission from the administration.)

* **IDEA #3** Cover 75 cafeteria chairs with a bright color. No chairs in your lunchroom? How about 15 tables to show how many kids died from gun violence.

* **IDEA #4** Have 75 kids paint half their face red. That'll get people's attention!

2 **GO EASY.** Think your school isn't going to go for any of these ideas? No worries. Here are some more subtle ideas that still send a powerful message:

* **IDEA #5** Have 75 students wear buttons with the words "I'm one in 75. Ask me what this means." This will start a dialogue, which is exactly what you want!

* **IDEA #6** Have 75 students carry a blue notebook (or whatever color you choose) across their chests that says "One in 75. Ask me what this means." Again, this will start discussion.

Violence & Bullying

155

I'M GOING TO TRY:

_____

_____

IF THAT DOESN'T WORK, I'LL TRY:

_____

_____

OR:

_____

_____

3 **PICK A DAY.** Check with the powers that be (principals, teachers, etc.) to make sure they're cool with your ideas and schedule a day. I'm going to do this on:

_____

4 **GET HELP.** Ask friends and classmates to help you out.

Helper #1's Name: _____

Contact Info: _____

Responsibilities: _____

Helper #2's Name: _____

Contact Info: _____

Responsibilities: _____

Helper #3's Name: _____

Contact Info: _____

Responsibilities: _____

5 **SPREAD THE WORD.** Make posters and flyers announcing the upcoming event so people know what's going on!

6 **GET THE FACTS.** The whole point is to raise awareness about gun violence. Make a Fact Sheet (see Project #11 on page 48) to hand out on the big day.

7 **THE BIG DAY.** Be energetic and enthusiastic. And make sure you and your team are prepared to answer people's questions. Check out Project #25 on page 197 so you're super-prepared.

8 **FOLLOW UP.** Get feedback from people. See what impacted them the most. Check in with your participants and ask them to share what they experienced and observed.

Did people think this was a cool project?

❑ YES ❑ NOT REALLY

THOUGHTS/OTHER IDEAS:

_____

_____

_____

_____

_____

_____

WHY OR WHY NOT:

_____
_____
_____
_____
_____
_____
_____

Did things go as planned?

❏ YES   ❏ NOT REALLY

Would you do this again?

❏ YES   ❏ NOT REALLY

IF SO, WHAT WOULD YOU DO DIFFERENTLY NEXT TIME?

_____
_____
_____
_____
_____
_____
_____

NOTES:

_____
_____
_____
_____
_____
_____
_____
_____
_____
_____
_____
_____
_____
_____
_____
_____
_____
_____
_____
_____
_____
_____
_____
_____
_____
_____
_____
_____
_____
_____
_____
_____
_____
_____

Violence & Bullying

WRITE AN ARTICLE ON CYBERBULLYING

Write an article for your school newspaper about cyberbullying. This is a great way to bring attention to this important issue! Here's how:

1 YOUR GOAL. First you need to decide what you want to accomplish with this article.

DISCUSS BULLYING IN MY SCHOOL?

☐ YES   ☐ NO

DISCUSS BULLYING IN SCHOOLS AROUND THE COUNTRY?

☐ YES   ☐ NO

MAKE A CHANGE IN MY SCHOOL?

☐ YES   ☐ NO

MAKE STUDENTS AWARE OF BULLYING?

☐ YES   ☐ NO

GIVE STUDENTS TOOLS TO HELP COMBAT BULLYING?

☐ YES   ☐ NO

---

2 GET A HEADLINE. A title is the first thing that a reader sees, so make it interesting!

EXAMPLE: CYBERBULLYING: A GROWING PROBLEM

MY TITLE IS:

_____
_____
_____
_____
_____

3 INVESTIGATE. Do you know anyone who has experienced cyberbullying? Listen to their stories and include them in your article. (You don't have to use their name if they don't want you to.)

THE STORIES I'M GOING TO USE:

_____
_____
_____
_____
_____

Violence & Bullying

4 **GET THE FACTS.** Statistics and facts help back up the points that you are trying to make (check out the box on page 49 for research tips).

HERE ARE SOME GOOD FACTS TO GET YOU STARTED:

★ Nine out of 10 middle school students have had their feelings hurt online.

★ Nearly 35 percent of kids have been threatened online, and almost one in five have had it happen more than once.

FIND MORE FACTS AT:

★ STOPCYBERBULLYING.ORG
★ DOSOMETHING.ORG/BOOK

5 **CLEAN IT UP.** Edit and spell-check before handing it in to the school newspaper. Get at least one person to read it. They can tell you if there's anything that sounds confusing.

6 **BE PREPARED.** Be ready to answer questions. Kids may ask you about your article, so be prepared for their questions. If you do Project #25 on page 197, you'll be ready for 'em!

NOTES:

WRITE LETTERS TO THE TROOPS

For soldiers deployed overseas, life can get a little lonely. Get your friends to join you in writing soldiers a few letters (three is a good number) and show them that you appreciate their service. Here's how:

I **GET WRITING.** Grab some paper and colored pencils or markers, then find an area where you can get to work. Even though you're writing to someone you've never met before, you can still write from the heart:

★ Address the soldier respectfully.

★ If you want, include a little about yourself like your age, your town, your favorite thing about America, or your favorite classes.

★ Thank them for their service.

★ Wish them a safe return home.

★ If you're comfortable with it, include your address or e-mail—sometimes soldiers will write you back!

YOUR LETTER MIGHT LOOK SOMETHING LIKE THIS:

2 **PERSONALIZE IT.** Draw pictures or include photos of your town, school, or family.

Dear Soldier,
Thank you for your service to America! My name is Michael and I am 11 years old. I live in Illinois with my Mom, Dad, sister Katie, and our dog Pepper. I am proud to live in a free country, and I am grateful that you are helping. I wish you a safe return home.
Best,
Michael
Springfield, Illinois
michael@yaboo.com

War & Peace

JUST REMEMBER:

★ You can't send food or candy.

★ You should not glue glitter or bulky items to the card.

3 SEND YOUR LETTERS. A Million Thanks is an organization that collects and sends letters to soldiers. Find a drop-off location online at:

AMILLIONTHANKS.ORG/DROP_OFF_LOCATIONS.ASP

IF THERE IS NO DROP-OFF SPOT NEAR YOU, SIMPLY MAIL THEM TO:

A Million Thanks
c/o DoSomething.org
17853 Santiago Blvd., #107-355
Villa Park, CA 92861

THEY'LL FORWARD THEM ALONG FOR YOU!

4 WANNA DO MORE? You can do this with friends every week or on the weekends. You could even set up a collection box at school so other people can add their notes. Or, send weekly e-mails through A Million Thanks. Check with their website to see how.

NOTES:

PROTEST THE USE OF CHILD SOLDIERS

Child soldiers, some as young as six, are fighting in conflicts around the world. Send special letters of protest to the countries that still don't forbid the use of child soldiers. Be part of Red Hand Day and include red handprints of all your friends with your letter—it's a great way to show support. Here's how:

1 GET THE OKAY. Get the principal's permission to host a Red Hand Day. Be sure to have your Elevator Pitch from Project #24 on page 193 ready.

❑ THE PRINCIPAL SAID YES
❑ THE PRINCIPAL SAID NO. THE REASONS HE/SHE GAVE:

_____
_____
_____

If the answer is no—don't worry: this is something you can do on your own!

2 GET YOUR SUPPLIES. Try your art teacher or someone in charge of the school's paint supply. You'll need:

❑ Red paint
❑ A paint roller
❑ Sheets of white paper

3 WHEN WILL YOU DO IT? February 12 is Red Hand Day, honoring the day the United Nations' child soldier restrictions went into effect. You could also choose May 25, the day the United Nations first adopted the protocol to restrict the use of child soldiers. Or any other day that seems right!

DATE OF MY RED HAND DAY:

_____

4 SPREAD THE WORD. Speak up during morning announcements or hang flyers around the school (with the school's permission). Make sure they contain the following info:

★ Red Hand Day is an international day to protest the use of child soldiers.

★ On Red Hand Day, students leave a painted handprint on a piece of paper along with a message against the use of child soldiers.

★ All you need is your hand and a pen to write your message.

★ The table will be located in [where] at [time of day] on [date].

★ Want to do more? Visit InvisibleChildren.org or UN.org's Cyber Schoolbus.

5 **THE BIG DAY.** When your classmates arrive to make their handprints, use the paint roller to color their hands red. Get them to make a handprint on a sheet of paper and add a personal message about why they want to end the use of child soldiers. Here are some examples:

★ "Children don't deserve to be in war."

★ "Everyone deserves to have a childhood."

★ "Children don't belong on the battlefield."

HAVE THE PERSON SIGN THEIR FIRST NAME AND THE NAME OF YOUR SCHOOL.

6 **WRITE IT UP.** Write a letter to send along with the red hands to the countries that have not yet ratified the protocol to ban child soldiers. The letter must urge them to do so as soon as possible. It should read something like this:

His/Her Excellency Mr./Ms. [Insert name]
Permanent Mission of [country] to the United Nations
[Address]

Your Excellency:

I am writing as a student at [name of school] in [city, state and country]. My classmates and I are concerned about the use of child soldiers around the world. We want to end a child's involvement in armed conflict, so we urge your government to ratify the Optional Protocol to the Convention on the Rights of the Child.

Thousands of child soldiers are fighting in dozens of conflicts worldwide. They are often forced or deceived into service, and as a soldier, they can see horrific violence. They may begin in noncombat roles like messengers, but often they can move into a combat role. Many do not survive.

Over 100 countries have ratified this treaty, which forbids the forced recruitment or service of children under the age of 18, but we want to see every country ratify the protocol. I have enclosed red handprints that show our commitment to stop the use of child soldiers. We ask your government to ratify the optional protocol and help to end the use of child soldiers.

Thank you very much for your consideration.

Sincerely yours,

[Your Signature]
[Your Name Typed or in Print]

War & Peace

163

7 SEND IT. Send your letter and the handprints to the United Nations office of the countries that have not pledged to end the use of child soldiers.

YOU CAN FIND THESE COUNTRIES' OFFICES AT:
REDHANDDAY.ORG/MEDIA-BOTSCHAFT SADRESSEN.PDF

8 SHOW OFF! Upload photos or videos of your event to Red Hand Day's website

WWW.REDHANDDAY.ORG

Tell them how many red hands you collected and how many United Nations missions you were able to contact.

THOUGHTS/IDEAS:

NOTES:

HOST A PICNIC FOR MILITARY FAMILIES

Over one million soldiers have served our country in Iraq and Afghanistan. That's a lot of absent moms and dads. Help create a support system for wives, husbands, and children of these soldiers. Host a picnic for those families in your area. Here's how:

1 **LOCATION, LOCATION, LOCATION.** You want to have enough room for people to run around, get loud, and get messy. You can try:

- ★ Public park
- ★ School field
- ★ Veterans Association
- ★ Lions Club or other civic organizations
- ★ Community center

I'D LIKE TO TRY:

_____

_____

IF THAT DOESN'T WORK, THEN I'LL TRY:

_____

_____

2 **CHOOSE THE DAY.** It needs to be warm! Weekends are the best, too.

DATE AND TIME OF THE PICNIC:

_____

3 **FIGURE OUT THE GUEST LIST.** Ask around the neighborhood for names of kids who have a deployed parent. Try to get their phone number or street address.

Call them or ring their doorbell. You could say:

> "Hello, my name is [name] and I'm hosting a picnic for families that have a loved one deployed overseas. Would you and your family be interested in attending the picnic on [date] at [time]?"

Ask them if they know other families who would like to be invited. Get their contact information. Watch your guest list grow!

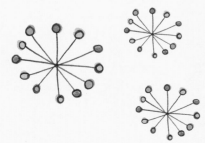

Keep track of your guest list ⟶

FAMILY	CONTACT INFORMATION	HOW MANY PEOPLE WILL ATTEND?

War & Peace

4 GET THE MENU. Ask each family to bring one dish or picnic supplies. Make sure that people are bringing a variety of stuff—you don't want four salads and no dessert!

FOOD/SUPPLY	FAMILY THAT WILL BRING IT
CUPS	
PLATES	
FORKS,SPOONS, AND KNIVES	
NAPKINS	
DRINKS	
SALADS	
SANDWICHES	
DESSERT	

5 THE BIG DAY. Say "hi" to each family as they arrive and thank them for coming. Once everyone arrives, make an announcement encouraging everyone to eat and exchange numbers or e-mail addresses.

6 BREAK THE ICE. Getting to know each other can be tricky. Host a game for the kids to help them relax. Pick a game for a large group. Here are some we like:

NEVER HAVE I EVER

Everyone sits in a circle around one person. The person in the middle will say something that they have never done (for example: "I have never tasted coconut water" or "I have never worn a dress"). All of the people who have never done that thing have to get up and run to find an empty seat in the circle, including the person in the middle. The person without a seat is now in the middle. Keep it going five or six times!

QUESTION BALL

Bring a large ball (a beach ball would work) and write at least 10 questions on it with a permanent marker. (For example, what's your favorite color? food? book? movie?) Get everyone in a circle and start the game by throwing the ball to a random person. Whatever question is under their right thumb is the question they have to answer!

OTHER GAME IDEAS:

_____
_____
_____
_____
_____

7 **CLEAN UP.** You don't want to leave your space a mess, so make sure everything is thrown away in trash cans after everyone is done. Get some friends to help!

WHO WILL HELP YOU WITH THIS?

Helper #1:

Helper #2:

Helper #3:

If you need more room, flip to page 268.

NOTES:

War & Peace

WANT TO BUILD YOUR OWN ACTION PLAN? COMPLETE PROJECTS #18—#22 TO FIGURE OUT THE

➡➡**HOW**

➡➡**WHAT**

➡➡**WHEN**

➡➡**WHERE**

➡➡**WHO**

IF YOU HAVE PICKED ONE OF THE ACTION PLANS FROM THE BOOK, USE THESE PROJECTS TO HELP YOU WORK OUT ALL THE DETAILS.

(Keep track of everything in Book It on page 263)

PROJECT #18: A ROUGH DRAFT

the HOW

I f you want to come up with your own foolproof plan, you'll need to make sure you nail down all the important details. You'll of course need to know *what* you want to do (duh!) but also *who* you want to do it with, *when* you're going to do it, and *where* it'll take place. You don't have to figure it out all at once—we'll take you through it step by step. But first, just take a stab at imagining *how* it might work.

> STUFF: Magazines, glue sticks, markers, crayons
>
> TIME: Enough time for you to get a visual of your project!

Say your goal is to increase the amount of recycling in your church by 50 percent. Your *what* could be to put five recycling bins around the church.

Okay, now you need to figure out the *how*. Close your eyes and picture the end result of your *what*: aluminum cans and plastic bottles in recycling bins. Work backward and get into the nuts and bolts. Where are those bins? Who do you imagine emptying those bins? Picture it all in your head and start putting the pieces together with a collage. Things will probably change, so think of this as your rough draft.

STEPS:

1. Put an image that represents your Thing in the middle of the paper. Is your Thing recycling? Put a picture of a soda can in the middle. Food for the homeless? Put a picture of a loaf of bread right in the middle.

2. *What* are you doing to take action? Collecting food? Raising money? Launching an awareness campaign? Find some images to represent these actions, and stick them around your Thing.

3. *Who* is helping you do it? Your friends? Do you need your principal's approval? Are you hoping the cheerleading squad turns up? Paste some photos of those peeps.

4. *When* is it happening? On a weekend? When it's warm outside?

5. *Where* are you doing it? At home? In school? Do you need a big outdoor space? Would your friend's yard work?

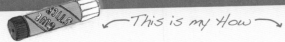

This is my How

The What

The Who

The When

The Where

TAKE IT TO THE NEXT LEVEL!

GRAB SOME POSTER BOARD AND MAKE IT POSTER-SIZED. ARE YOU DREAMING EVEN BIGGER?

PROJECT #19: TARGET THE RIGHT TIME

Timing is everything. Finding the perfect moment to launch your Action Plan can make or break it (if you're planning to sell ice-cold lemonade to raise money for your Thing, the dead of winter may not be the best time, right?). If you want to organize a river cleanup, Earth Day (April 22) would be a nice fit.

There's a lot to consider: the weather, your schedule (are you going to have enough time to do something during soccer season?), or if you can tie the event to a special holiday. Check with your parents to see if there's anything big coming up that you might not know about—like your grandparents' 50th wedding anniversary or a surprise trip around the world (hey, you can dream, right?). Once you know what works for you, figure out what works best for the project. Use the chart on the next page to zero in on your "when."

STEPS:

> **STUFF:** Pen or pencil, your schedule
>
> **TIME:** Not too long. But give it some thought.

1. Pick a season. Is it warm or cold? Indoors or outdoors? If it's warm out, that nixes winter, right? If it's in school, that nixes summertime. Get it? Circle the season in the chart opposite.

2. Pick a month. You picked the season, so that eliminates some months, right? (Check out the calendar on pages 174–175 for some inspiration.) Circle the months that could work.

3. Pick a time frame. Is your Action Plan a one-time thing? A month-long campaign? Circle the correct box.

4. Pick a day. What days work best for you and your crew? Do you have a quiz every Wednesday in science class that you cram for the night before? Then cross out Tuesday. Then pick a time.

5. Pick a time of day. When are people around to help and participate? When are you full of energy? What time of day fits your Thing best? If you're doing a bake sale, lunchtime could be just right.

Season
(circle one)

(FALL)   (WINTER)   (SPRING)   (SUMMER)

Month
(circle one)

SEPTEMBER   DECEMBER   MARCH   JUNE

OCTOBER   JANUARY   APRIL   JULY

NOVEMBER   FEBRUARY   MAY   AUGUST

Time frame
(circle one)

ONE DAY ONLY   MULTIPLE DAYS

Day(s)
(circle any)

SUN   MON   TUES   WED   THURS   FRI   SAT

Time of day (circle one)

MORNING   AFTERNOON   EVENING

173

NATIONAL EMERGENCY PREPAREDNESS WEEK (Week of September 11) Use the anniversary of September 11, 2001, to prepare your community for future disasters, both natural and man-made. Make an evacuation plan for your house. Learn how on page 101.

INTERNATIONAL DAY OF PEACE (September 21) Celebrate peace with those most impacted by war. Organize a picnic for military families. See how on pages 165–167.

NATIONAL DIABETES MONTH Twenty-four-million children and adults in the U.S. live with diabetes. Ask your school to have a sugar-free lunch day to raise awareness about the disease. Write up a Fact Sheet with important facts about the disease to hand out at lunchtime. Get tips on making Fact Sheets in Project #11 on page 48.

BREAST CANCER AWARENESS MONTH Breast cancer is the most common cancer among women in the U.S. Ask your whole class to participate and make a collage of all the people you know who have been touched by breast cancer.

AMERICA RECYCLES DAY (November 15) Set up a recycling system at your home or improve the existing system. Learn how on page 116.

THANKSGIVING DAY (Third Thursday in November) This holiday is all about food so it's a great day to focus on hunger-related projects. See pages 130–131 and pages 136–137.

WINTER COAT DRIVE It's getting cold out there. Hold a coat drive at school and pass on the donations to a local homeless shelter. Learn how on pages 149–152.

WORLD HUMAN RIGHTS DAY (December 10) The United Nations has declared December 10 World Human Rights Day. It's a great day for a poster drive to raise awareness about the Universal Declaration of Human Rights. Learn how on pages 142–143.

NATIONAL STAYING HEALTHY MONTH Put your New Year's resolutions into action! Get your community in shape by planning a fun run or walk.

MARTIN LUTHER KING DAY (Third Monday in January) A day to celebrate the life (and birthday) of civil rights leader Martin Luther King Jr. Remind people of his amazing accomplishments by holding a poster campaign of Dr. King's famous quotes. Learn how on pages 102–103.

BLACK HISTORY MONTH History can be a great teacher. Give a presentation during a school assembly about influential black leaders who fought discrimination. Get tips on giving presentations on pages 90–93. Or, organize a poetry reading (see pages 106–107).

RED HAND DAY (February 12) Protest the use of child soldiers in conflicts around the world. Get details on giving presentations on pages 162–164.

AMERICAN RED CROSS MONTH The Red Cross has been helping people in disaster areas since 1881. Celebrate this great American organization with a disaster kit supply drive. Get tips on how to have a collection drive on pages 94, 108, 127, 132, 149.

VOW OF SILENCE DAY (March 1) Take a vow of silence and raise awareness about kids around the world who are denied their basic human rights. Can't make it a whole day? Ask your homeroom teacher to let your class have a five-minute moment of silence before the end of class. Learn how on pages 140–141.

KEEP AMERICA BEAUTIFUL MONTH Clean up a street or stretch of river and keep your portion of the country beautiful. Learn how to organize a cleanup on pages 119–121.

EARTH DAY (April 22) It's the official day to think about how to save the earth, so help your school plan their Earth Day activities and commit to protecting the environment. Get ideas on pages 116–121.

ASTHMA AND ALLERGY AWARENESS MONTH Asthma and allergies are the most common chronic diseases among kids. Have a visual art show and charge admission to raise money for the Asthma and Allergy Foundation of America. Get tips on pages 112–113.

HURRICANE AWARENESS WEEK (Last full week in May) Even if you don't live in a hurricane-prone area, you can still raise money to help victims of hurricanes and natural disasters. Organize a Penny War to raise money at school. Learn how on pages 144–148.

WORLD REFUGEE DAY (June 20). Hold a bake sale to raise money for UNICEF's work with children living in refugee camps around the world. Get the details on holding a bake sale on pages 98–100. Check out www.unicef.org for donation information.

NATIONAL RECREATION AND PARKS MONTH Celebrate the outdoors and all the summer has to offer in July. Volunteer at a local a park or recreation center to help them with a park cleanup. Learn how on pages 119–121.

NATIONAL LITERACY DAY (July 2) Hold a book drive for a library that needs to stock its shelves. Get tips on how to have a drive on pages 94, 108, 127, 132, and 149.

WATER QUALITY MONTH More than 1 in 6 people in the world doesn't have access to clean drinking water. Hold a car wash and raise money to bring clean water to a town in Africa. Visit www.thewaterproject.org for more information.

NATIONAL HOMELESS ANIMALS DAY (August 16) Spend a weekend walking dogs at an animal rescue shelter. Learn how on pages 86–87.

THEY'RE DOING SOMETHING!

NAME: Max Wallack, 13, Massachusetts
THING: Alzheimer's Disease

KEEP YOUR BRAIN ALIVE!
Max's Thing is helping the elderly. When he was six, he invented the Great Granny Booster Step to help disabled people get into high vehicles, like minivans. After his great-grandma died of Alzheimer's, he started Puzzles to Remember, a not-for-profit organization which collects puzzles for nursing homes. He has given more than 1,800 puzzles to about 80 health-care facilities. Check him out at: DoSomething.org/book.

NAME: Alicia Keys
THING: AIDS/HIV

HELPING KIDS WITH AIDS
Alicia Keys took a trip to Africa and saw the illness and death caused by AIDS firsthand. She says, "I got sad and mad and had to harness my sadness and anger into action!" She started her own organization, Keep a Child Alive, to help kids with AIDS get medicine and medical care.

PROJECT #20: LOCATION, LOCATION, LOCATION

Where you want to do your Thing depends on three things: 1) How visible you want to be; 2) How many people will be participating; 3) How much noise you are going to make. If you're having a fund-raiser or awareness event like a bake sale, a car wash, or a battle of the bands, you'll want to plan to be in a place that gets a lot of foot traffic and can fit a lot of people. If you're having a collection drive (coats, canned food, school supplies, etc.), you want to think about spots that get crowded, such as churches, malls, schools, town halls. If you're looking for a quieter setting, say a discussion about discrimination at school, think smaller—living rooms, empty classrooms, your backyard.

> **STUFF:** Pens, markers, crayons, magazines, poster board (optional)
>
> **TIME:** Long enough to see your *where* in your mind

STEPS:

1. First, figure out the amount of space you will need. Are you going to need lots of room? Do you want a quiet space where people can reflect upon your Thing? Check out the box on page 178 for some ideas.

2. What kind of foot traffic will you need? Does the town hall attract enough people? Maybe the supermarket entrance would be better? Are your posters going to get more attention on the library bulletin board or at the coffee shop?

3. Another thing to consider is noise level. Are you having a moment of silence? A candlelight vigil? Pick a secluded (but easy-to-get-to) area where serenity can reign supreme. Want to breathe fire into your Thing and watch people get wild at a rally? Try a public park where it doesn't matter how loud you get.

4. Remember to call or set up a meeting to make sure your location is available, affordable, big enough, and that you have permission to use it.

GOOD FOR A BIG GROUP

- ★ Auditorium
- ★ Town hall
- ★ Community center
- ★ Basketball court
- ★ Place of worship
- ★ Movie theater
- ★ Cafeteria

QUIET PLACES

- ★ Classroom
- ★ Your house (or a friend's house)
- ★ Coffee shop
- ★ Bookstore

LOTS OF FOOT TRAFFIC

- ★ Public park
- ★ Supermarket entrance
- ★ Public swimming pool
- ★ Mall

You could go big...

... or small

Take some notes about your event

Crowd: ❏ Big   ❏ Small

Foot traffic: ❏ A lot   ❏ A little   ❏ None

Noise level: ❏ We'll be loud   ❏ We'll be quiet

The perfect location:

If I can't go there, I'll try:

or maybe:

Contact info:

PROJECT #21: CASTING CALL

Ever heard the phrase "There's power in numbers"? Well, it's true. The more people are involved, the bigger the impact. You could do a lot of amazing things on your own, but imagine if there were two of you. Or even ten of you! Even if you're working solo, it's likely that you'll need to rely on or reach out to people to get the job done. This project is going to help you get a picture of who you're going to need.

Imagine that your Action Plan is a movie and you're the director (and the star!). You have a great script, you've picked the location, and now it's time to get the cast together. It takes more than actors to make a movie, so don't forget the behind-the-scenes folks.

STUFF: Pen and a vivid imagination

TIME: As long as it takes to get that Oscar! Just kidding. But long enough to figure out the cast and crew.

STEPS:

1. If your project was a movie, what kind would it be? Is it a movie with just a few characters or a big 3-D spectacle with tons of people and special effects? Or maybe it's a one-man show?

2. Look at the list of classic movie character types on the opposite page and think about whether they belong in your movie. If they do, about how many are there?

3. Start thinking about who you might cast in these roles. Fill in the names in the space provided.

THE HERO/HEROINE (THAT'S YOU!)

What will you be in charge of?

THE VILLAIN

Make this the problem you're trying to solve.

THE SIDEKICKS

Every Batman needs his Robin. Do you need a right-hand guy or girl? Or five?

THE WIZARDS

Need permissions? Need access? Who are the powerful people who will help make it happen?

THE CREW

This is your behind-the-scenes team. Is someone driving you around? Who's making the posters?

PROJECT #22: MATCHMAKER

N ow that you know what kind of help you need, here comes the tricky part—assigning responsibilities. You want to match people's skills with the task, but you also want to make sure they are happy with their assignment. You may think your friend would be great leading the setup team, but he wants to do the posters. It's important that your friends are happy while they're helping out, because it means they won't want to stop! So why not give them a say?

STEPS:

STUFF: Pen or marker, paper

TIME: If it's a nice day, as long as you want!

1. Have your friends answer the questions on the next page.

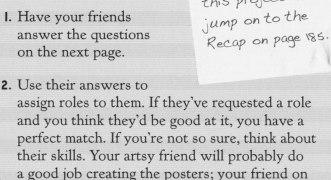
If you're working solo, just skip this project and jump on to the Recap on page 185.

2. Use their answers to assign roles to them. If they've requested a role and you think they'd be good at it, you have a perfect match. If you're not so sure, think about their skills. Your artsy friend will probably do a good job creating the posters; your friend on student government would be great at getting people to sign a petition.

3. Don't forget to check in with your friends to make sure everyone is happy with his or her job. You may have to do some rearranging, but that's better than having an unhappy team member.

What do you like to do when you're hanging out or messing around?

What do you think your strengths are?

Why do you want to help?

If your team members are up for it (and you think they can handle the responsibility), tap a few vice-presidents and put them in ↙

charge of entire parts of the project. You can let them do their Thing, but check in on a regular basis to make sure things are moving along.

How do you want to help?

WHAT MAKES A GOOD LEADER?

A LEADER MOTIVATES. No one is more pumped about your Thing than you—let that energy inspire your team.

A LEADER IS A TEAM PLAYER. This project isn't about you—it's about doing something big, together.

A LEADER PLANS. Be ready for the expected *and* unexpected. Be organized, be prepared, but stay flexible.

A LEADER IS HONEST. Lying to your team (even white lies) is the fastest way to make them mad. Not worth it.

A LEADER IS CREATIVE. Sometimes this means taking risks or doing something that might be unpopular.

A LEADER IS RESPONSIBLE. Make sure you dot all your i's and cross your t's, and don't blame others if something goes wrong.

A LEADER COMMUNICATES. Don't make people read your mind—be clear about what you need and choose your words wisely.

A LEADER LISTENS. You won't always have the answer, but someone on your team might—so pay attention.

Hey! If you've brought together a great team, start a Do Something Club and make it official! Find out how at:

DOSOMETHING.ORG/BOOK

build it

WOW, YOU'VE BUILT A ROCK-SOLID PLAN! YOU FIGURED OUT ALL THE PIECES THAT WILL MAKE YOUR PROJECT—WHATEVER IT IS!—AN AMAZING SUCCESS. YOU KNOW WHAT YOU'RE GOING TO DO, WHERE YOU'RE GOING TO DO IT, WHEN IT'LL TAKE PLACE, **AND WHO'S GOING TO HELP**. YOU'RE READY TO TAKE IT TO THE NEXT LEVEL. YOU'RE READY TO PULL IT OFF. SO WHAT'S STOPPING YOU? **TURN THE PAGE AND DO IT!**

RECAP

CHAPTER 4

do it!

SEEING A PROBLEM IS GREAT. BELIEVING YOU CAN MAKE A DIFFERENCE IS REALLY IMPORTANT. BUILDING A ROCK-SOLID PLAN WILL HELP YOU BE INCREDIBLY EFFECTIVE. **BUT NOTHING MATTERS MORE THAN ACTUALLY GETTING OUT THERE AND DOING IT.**

YOU CAN READ AND WRITE ABOUT RIDING A HORSE, BUT AT SOME POINT YOU NEED TO GET ON AND ACTUALLY RIDE IT, RIGHT? PULLING OFF YOUR ACTION PLAN MEANS SPREADING THE WORD, GETTING MORE PEOPLE TO SIGN ON TO HELP, STAYING ORGANIZED, FOCUSED, AND INSPIRED. IT'S NOT ALWAYS GOING TO BE EASY——YOU HAVE TO PREPARE FOR THE UNEXPECTED! BUT YOU'VE COME TOO FAR TO STOP NOW. IT'S TIME FOR YOU TO **DO IT.**

THESE ARE THE QUESTIONS YOU NEED TO ANSWER!

HOW DO I STAY FOCUSED?

HOW DO I DESCRIBE MY THING TO OTHER PEOPLE?

HOW DO I SPREAD THE WORD?

DO PROJECTS #23 — #34 TO FIGURE IT OUT!

HOW DO I STAY ORGANIZED?

HOW DO I MANAGE MY TEAM?

HOW DO I STAY POSITIVE?

PROJECT #23: ON A MISSION

A mission statement describes the purpose of your project clearly and simply. Why is it important? Because it keeps you (and your team, if you have one) focused on your goal. It doesn't include personal info and it's not warm and fuzzy. A mission statement describes your plan and includes a goal so you'll know when you've reached the finish line . . . and it's only one sentence long! That's right—one sentence. That's all you need! Take, for example, Kiva, an organization that allows people to lend money via the Internet to entrepreneurs in developing countries. Its mission statement: **"To connect people through lending for the sake of alleviating poverty."** How simple is that? Clear. To the point. One sentence. Now it's your turn!

> **STUFF:** A pen and your team (if you have one)
>
> **TIME:** Enough time for you to create a genius one-sentence mission statement

STEPS:

1. Brainstorm the questions on the scratchpad on page 191. List any and all words, phrases, or ideas that come to mind.

2. Try filling in the blanks:

   Our mission is to _____ the _____
   [VERB]   [POPULATION YOU'RE TRYING TO HELP]
   of _____ by _____.
   [LOCATION]   [WHAT YOU'RE EXACTLY DOING]

   Example: "Our mission is to help the homeless youth of Orange County by collecting 500 jeans for our local youth shelter."

3. Read your mission statement to at least five people. Do they understand what you're trying to do? If not, get their feedback and make a few changes. Maybe you need to scrap the whole thing and start all over! No biggie. You'd rather get it right, right?

4. Write your shiny new mission statement on page 192. Doesn't that feel good?

Some MISSION STATEMENTS we love:

ASPCA provides effective means for the prevention of cruelty to animals throughout the United States.

UNITED WAY improves lives by mobilizing the caring power of communities.

THE AMERICAN RED CROSS is a humanitarian organization, led by volunteers, that provides relief to victims of disasters and helps people prevent, prepare for, and respond to emergencies.

HABITAT FOR HUMANITY seeks to eliminate poverty housing and homelessness from the world and to make decent shelter a matter of conscience and action.

THE VH1 SAVE THE MUSIC FOUNDATION is a nonprofit organization dedicated to restoring instrumental music education in American public schools, and raising awareness about the importance of music as part of each child's complete education.

THE NATURAL RESOURCES DEFENSE COUNCIL works to protect wildlife and wild places and to ensure a healthy environment for all life on earth.

AMNESTY INTERNATIONAL conducts research and generates action to prevent and end grave abuses of human rights and to demand justice for those whose rights have been violated.

DOCTORS WITHOUT BORDERS organizes volunteer doctors and nurses to provide urgent medical care to victims of war and disaster regardless of race, religion, or politics.

MISSION STATEMENT
SCRATCHPAD

What/whose needs are you
trying to address?

What are you doing to
address those needs?

MY MISSION STATEMENT:

Some MISSION STATEMENT tips:

- You and your team should believe in your statement
- Make sure everyone gets a say
- Be clear and realistic
- Avoid emotional language
- Include a concrete goal
- Keep it short and simple

PROJECT #24:
ELEVATOR PITCH

You know that what you're doing is important, but can you convince other people that it's important? Getting your message out there and getting other people to care about your Thing is essential if you want your plan to be a success. That's why you need to find the right words to talk about your Thing. You started doing this with your mission statement, but now it's time to expand on that one sentence.

What if you were riding in an elevator with an adult who could help get your plan off the ground? You have only a few moments before the person gets off—could you describe your Thing in under a minute? If your answer is no, that's okay. That's what this next project will help you to figure out.

STEPS:

1. Fill in the blanks on page 194.

> **STUFF:** A pen and your noggin
>
> **TIME:** More than a minute, but it'll be worth it!

2. List up to three things you want people to know about your Thing and why it's important to you. Try to be really specific and use some strong facts. (Check out that Fact Sheet from Project #11 on page 48.)

3. Let them know why you're giving them the pitch in the first place. Do you need something from them? A donation? Permissions? Do you want them to volunteer? Make sure you know what you're asking for before you start pitching.

4. Find an adult to practice on (and bring a stopwatch). Don't worry if you don't get it right the first time—ask for feedback and give it another go.

SAMPLE ELEVATOR PITCH

Hi. My name is Alex Maste. I'm in the 5th grade at Hillside Middle School.

I'm working on doing something for homeless kids in our state by holding a clothing drive at school.

This is important to me because a lot of homeless kids struggle with trying to fit in at school and many are bullied because of what they wear. One in three homeless people in the U.S. is under 18, so this is a pretty big problem.

I could use your help in driving the donations to the local homeless shelter. Is this something you could do?

Fill in the blanks for your own pitch here!

MY ELEVATOR PITCH

Hi. My name is _____

I am in the _____ grade in _____
_____ School.

I'm working on doing something about
_____
_____

This is important to me because
_____
_____
_____
_____

I could use your help in _____
_____
_____
_____
_____
_____

This last line could change, depending on who you're talking to, so be prepared.

* Your pitch can come in handy outside of elevators, too. Use it to help you figure out what to say on your school's PA system during morning announcements, or in a letter to your senators.

THEY'RE DOING SOMETHING!

NAME: *Jordan Coleman, 14, New Jersey*
THING: *Education*

ACTION!
Jordan was angry when he learned that fewer than half of African American boys graduate high school. He's an actor, so he decided to make a movie called *Say It Loud* to raise awareness about the importance of education. He toured with the film to spread his message to young people in community centers and schools around the country. He even got to speak at an education rally during the Presidential Inauguration of 2009! Check him out at: DoSomething.org/book.

NAME: *Tony Hawk*
THING: *Health & Fitness*

OLLIES AND KICKFLIPS ALLOWED!
When he's not catching air at the skate park, Tony is making sure other young skateboarders have the same opportunities he had as a kid. His foundation helps build skate parks in communities across the country where young people and at-risk youth can hang out. It goes beyond just boarding, though—his skate parks gives kids a place to gather, even in dangerous cities.

PROJECT #25: DEBATE CLUB

Now that you have your one-minute Elevator Pitch, you're a lean, mean, smooth-talking machine. But what happens if the person you're pitching to asks you a question (or five)? Will you be ready? There's no way to predict what people will ask, but you can go into the conversation prepared. Find your bossiest, most know-it-all friend or older sibling and ask them to challenge you to a debate. Don't get scared—it's not a fight! A debate is just a simple discussion where two people challenge each other to think about things in a new way. Remember: You chose your Thing because it's something you care about. Take that passion into the debate with you, and you'll rock it!

STEPS:

STUFF: Pencil, question list, bossy friend

TIME: Depends how persuasive you are

1. With your debate partner, come up with a list of 11 questions you think people might ask. What were some of the questions YOU had when you were researching your Thing back in Chapter 2, "Believe It"?

2. Have your debate partner come up with a surprise question—this will keep you on your toes!

3. Sit on opposite ends of a big table.

4. Your debate partner will ask you questions and rate you on a few things:
   * Did you make sense?
   * Did you give enough info?
   * Did you convince him/her?

5. Write down the question that was the toughest to answer and then write down how you plan to respond to it. Now you have the start of a rock-solid argument.

Write down eleven questions you think people might ask you about your Thing.

11 QUESTIONS

1.

2.

3.

4.

5.

6.

7.

8.

9.

10.

11.

Let your partner rate how well you answered the five toughest questions.

DEBATE SCORECARD

Question #1: _____
_____
_____

Did your partner's answer make sense to you? ___Yes ___ No

Did your partner give you enough info? ___Yes ___ No

Were you convinced by your partner's answer? ___Yes ___ No

DEBATE SCORECARD

Question #2: _____
_____
_____

Did your partner's answer make sense to you? ___Yes ___ No

Did your partner give you enough info? ___Yes ___ No

Were you convinced by your partner's answer? ___Yes ___ No

DEBATE SCORECARD

Question #3: _____
_____
_____

Did your partner's answer make sense to you? ___Yes ___ No

Did your partner give you enough info? ___Yes ___ No

Were you convinced by your partner's answer? ___Yes ___ No

DEBATE SCORECARD

Question #4: _____
_____
_____

Did your partner's answer make sense to you? ___Yes ___No
Did your partner give you enough info? ___Yes ___No
Were you convinced by your partner's answer? ___Yes ___No

DEBATE SCORECARD

Question #5: _____
_____
_____

Did your partner's answer make sense to you? ___Yes ___No
Did your partner give you enough info? ___Yes ___No
Were you convinced by your partner's answer? ___Yes ___No

DEBATE SCORECARD

SURPRISE QUESTION!: _____
_____
_____

Did your partner's answer make sense to you? ___Yes ___No
Did your partner give you enough info? ___Yes ___No
Were you convinced by your partner's answer? ___Yes ___No

PROJECT #26: MAKE IT FLOW

The rough draft of your Do Something Plan has all the pieces, but it was mostly big-picture stuff. Now that you're out there doing your Thing, you'll find that there are a lot of details that you need to keep track of.

A Flow Chart is a great way to keep track of all these mini-goals and to-dos. By breaking down the things you need to accomplish into itty-bitty pieces, your goal will seem totally manageable.

STEPS:

> **STUFF:** A pen or pencil
>
> **TIME:** This might take a while, or it might go super fast—just go with the flow!

1. Insert your goal at the top of page 203.

2. Start breaking down what you need into small pieces. Think about ways you plan to accomplish your goal and list the tools you need to get it done.

3. Do that for each item until you've brought it down to the most basic level.

4. Tear out your Flow Chart and hang it in your locker or in your room so you remember everything you need to do!

5. Keep track of all the details in "Book It" beginning on page 263.

GOAL:

GET 25 KIDS TO GO TO AN AFTER-SCHOOL SCREENING OF *AN INCONVENIENT TRUTH*, FOLLOWED BY A DISCUSSION ABOUT GLOBAL WARMING.

GET PERMISSION TO RESERVE A ROOM
(keep your permissions organized on page 269)

SPREAD THE WORD!

GET SUPPLIES AND MATERIALS FOR THE SCREENING.

Talk to the person in charge of tech at school about reserving and setting up video equipment.

Bring snacks for everybody?

Make copies of my global warming Fact Sheet.

Get permission from the principal to hold the screening!

Can we get someone to donate some chips and drinks? Talk to cafeteria staff.

Make posters to hang in the cafeteria and around school.

Make an announcement during assembly or over the PA.

Make stickers with my group's slogan.

Ask team to come up with 3 ideas about what should go on the posters.

Get supplies: poster board, markers, pics, etc.

Schedule a time to make the announcement.

Put the 3 things that have to happen first on the top yellow, green, and pink cards.

MY GOAL:

CHECK OUT
DOSOMETHING.ORG/BOOK
FOR MORE: _blank_
Flow Charts

203

PROJECT #27:
GET 'EM TOGETHER

If you brought a team on board to help you accomplish the plan, you'll want to get them all together at least once before the special day. What for? To make sure they know exactly what they've signed up for and what you expect of them. You're going to organize a meeting!

     A meeting may sound like a really adult thing to do, but it doesn't have to be hard and it doesn't have to be boring. As long as you're organized and plan some fun stuff to mix in with the business talk, you might actually have a good time! Start planning!

STEPS:

1. Send out an e-mail or call your team to set up a time to meet, at least one week in advance.

> **STUFF:** Sign-in sheet, pens, name tags, Elevator Pitch, Fact Sheet
>
> **TIME:** Under an hour

2. Make copies of your Fact Sheet from Project #11 on page 48 and your Flow Chart from Project #26 on page 203. If it's a big group, name tags would be a good idea (everyone can decorate their own!); also have a sign-in sheet where everybody writes their phone numbers and e-mail addresses.

3. Write up a meeting agenda so you stay focused and don't run too long (check out the example on the opposite page). Try to keep the meeting under an hour. People will start to get fidgety!

Sample Meeting Agenda

PURPOSE OF MEETING: To discuss poster campaign

WHEN: Saturday, May 11, 1:30 p.m.

WHERE: Sam's house (231 Montague Avenue)

PARTICIPANTS: Maisie, Nell, Jonas, Isaac, Bess, Matthew, and Sam

AGENDA ITEMS:

1:30–1:35 p.m. Introduction *Try the icebreaker on page 206.*

1:35–2:00 p.m. Get to know each other

2:00–2:20 p.m. Discuss the plan

2:20–2:25 p.m. Question-and-answer time

2:25–2:45 p.m. Assign responsibilities

2:45–3:00 p.m. Recap and wrap-up

THE FLOW OF A MEETING

1. **INTRODUCTION.** Present yourself and your Thing but save the details for later. Just stick to your Elevator Pitch (see Project #24 on page 193). Thank everyone for coming.

2. **GET TO KNOW EACH OTHER.** Have everyone introduce themselves (even if they already know each other!). If people are being shy, try an icebreaker—see the note below for details.

3. **EXPLAIN YOUR ACTION PLAN.** This is your chance to get into the nitty-gritty of your Thing: why you chose it, what you're doing about it, and how they can help. Hand out copies of your Flow Chart so people can see what needs to get done.

4. **QUESTION-AND-ANSWER TIME.** Give your team a chance to ask questions and make suggestions. Smart friends are the best!

5. **ASSIGN RESPONSIBILITIES.** Pass around your list of to-dos and have everyone sign up for a different task. If someone isn't sure, assign him a task. This can be tricky. Check out Project #22 on page 182 for some tips.

6. **RECAP AND WRAP-UP.** Sum up the details of your Plan and remind everyone of their responsibilities. And say thank you, again!

An icebreaker is a warm-up activity that helps loosen everyone up and get them in the mood to tackle the project. Try the Skittle game. As the kids enter the room, have them take a handful of candy but tell them not to eat it just yet. (You should take some, too.) For each Skittle they take, the kids need to say one thing about themselves. You can add a twist by assigning a category to each color: For example, orange = cause that matters to you, red = best trip you ever took, green = something about your family, blue = favorite hobby.

YOUR Meeting Agenda

PURPOSE OF MEETING:

WHEN:

WHERE:

PARTICIPANTS:

AGENDA ITEMS:

Note how long you want to spend on each thing.

_____ Introduction

_____ Get to know each other

_____ Discuss the plan

_____ Question-and-answer time

_____ Assign responsibilities

_____ Recap and wrap-up

DISAGREEMENTS HAPPEN!
HOW DO YOU DEAL WITH THEM?

1. Give people time to calm down.

2. Listen. Let each person explain his or her point of view or feelings.

3. Let them know that friends don't always agree but they do have to respect each others' ideas.

4. Remind them that they are doing something really important—disagreements shouldn't get in the way of getting the job done.

TAKE IT TO THE NEXT LEVEL!

ASK A FRIEND TO SERVE AS SECRETARY FOR THE MEETING. HIS/HER ONLY JOB WILL BE TO TAKE NOTES AT THE MEETING, WHICH ARE CALLED THE "MINUTES"—A WRITTEN ACCOUNT OF WHAT HAPPENED AT THE MEETING, THE ACTIONS ASSIGNED, AND DECISIONS MADE. MINUTES SHOULD INCLUDE:

1. DATE AND TIME
2. PURPOSE OF THE MEETING
3. ASSIGNMENTS MADE
4. DECISIONS MADE
5. STEPS FOR FOLLOWING UP

PROJECT #28: NAME IT!

You have a great cause, a great project, and (for some of you) a great team. Now you need a great name. Naming your project or group gives it an identity and lets people know what you're all about. If you're working in a team, a name is a way to unify the group. If you're working solo, it's an easy way to let people know that working for your Thing is more than just a hobby (so instead of everyone calling your thing "Caleb's Project," they'll call it by its official name, "Ocean Salvation Group," or "OSG" for short. Sounds much more serious, right?).

STEPS:

1. You are going to create a mind map. Write down your Thing in a circle in the middle of page 211. Draw lines coming from the circle and write down the words and images that come to mind when you think about your Thing. (Check out the sample on the next page.)

> **STUFF:** Pen, pencil, paper
>
> **TIME:** Give yourself at least 15 minutes for the mind map; take all the time you need for brainstorming

2. Think about who you're working with, who you're trying to help. If your project was an object, what would it smell like, taste like, feel like? Don't be afraid to go a little nuts.

3. Highlight the words on the map that best capture what you think is most important about your project or group. Keep an eye out for words with only one or two syllables, or strong action words like "Fight!" "Save!" "End!"

4. Start stringing together various combinations of words. Don't be afraid to experiment with different styles. You could go for something catchy, playing with words from your mind map like "The Green Wings," if your thing is the environment. Or something straightforward like "Youth for Human Rights," or something powerful and energetic like "End War Now!"

hybrid cars

solar panels

energy efficiency

acid rain

ozone

smog

asthma

whales

ocean

feathers

wings

birds

dollars

grass

green

envy

recycle

pollution

animals

nature

roots

environment

trees

flowers

earth

dirt

spring

mother

sun

globe

global warming

climate change

ozone

green   wings

YOUR Mind Map
↓

My group's name is:

TAKE IT TO THE NEXT LEVEL!

NOW THAT YOU HAVE A NAME, MAKE IT
ULTRA-OFFICIAL WITH A SNAZZY LOGO!
(SEE THE NEXT PROJECT.)

PROJECT #29: LOGO POGO

CHECK OUT
DOSOMETHING.ORG/BOOK
FOR: a cool logo
generator

A logo is the most recognizable part of an organization's identity. Think about Apple's simple apple logo, MTV's cool block letters, and Disney's castle logo (a combination of Walt Disney's signature and the castle from *Sleeping Beauty*). Habitat for Humanity uses an image of people under a roof and the United Way's logo features a figure jumping in the palm of a big hand.

These logos may be very different, but they all accomplish the same thing: They send an instant visual message about what their organization or brand is all about. Your logo is a lot like your Elevator Pitch, only you want your ideas to go to people's eyes instead of their ears. Is your project serious? Is it fun? Is it hip? A logo can reflect all of these things.

STEPS:

STUFF: Mind map, pens, markers, computer (optional)

TIME: This one is fun—take as long as you want!

1. Brainstorm an image or a symbol that could represent your group or project. Look at the mind map you made in the last Project. Do any strong images jump out at you?

2. Take your project or group name and try to write it in an interesting way. Experiment with size, capitalization, and font style.

3. Pick a color! Pick a few! You want your colors to relate to your group's purpose. Say your project is about organic farming so you choose brown—the color of dirt. If you're an antidiscrimination activism group, you could pick a rainbow!

4. If you're using an image, place it so it fits with the name visually. You can write it around the image, inside the image, or simply place it next to, above, or below the image. Mess around with the logo on the computer, or just with a pencil and paper, if that's more your style.

HOW OUR LOGO WORKS:

The fun, blocky font reflects our bold attitude.

Stacked words keep it compact.

Our name is energetic and to the point.

Start thinking about your logo by answering these questions

When I think about my Thing, these images pop up:

When I search for my Thing on the Internet, these images pop up:

When I look my Thing up in books, I see a lot of:

Now start sketching!

When I doodle, I draw pictures that relate to my Thing, like this:

Choose your favorite doodle and fine-tune it!

Here is my logo!

TAKE IT TO THE NEXT LEVEL!

IF YOUR LOGO NEEDS SOME MORE TWEAKING TO MAKE IT LOOK MORE "POLISHED," ASK A FRIEND WHO'S A REALLY GOOD ARTIST TO HELP YOU PERFECT YOUR SKETCH!

PROJECT #30: SPREAD THE WORD

You want to spread the word about your Thing or event, right? A great way to do this is to create flyers. They can be colorful and eye-catching while giving some important facts about your Thing. Think about it—when you got started looking into facts about your Thing, you got energized—you got mad, you got psyched, you got inspired to do something!

Flyers come in handy in a lot of different situations— hand them out at meetings, use them to raise awareness about your Thing, or advertise your event. You can post them around school or ask the town newspaper to include one in the next issue. Or how about your school or town's website? Think big! Why not? It's for a good cause.

STUFF: Paper, pens, markers, your Fact Sheets, poster board

TIME: Enough to get the facts on the page looking good

STEPS:

1. Come up with an attention-grabbing headline or slogan (see the box on page 220 for some ideas).

2. Find a great image that grabs people's attention.

3. A few facts about your Thing. Take a look at the Fact Sheet you made in Project #11 on page 48.

4. Include details on what action you want people to take. If you want them to write to an elected official (like a senator or governor), give them the address where they can send the letter. If you want them to come to an event, make sure you include all the details.

Sample flyer

THEY'RE NOT HUMANS, BUT THEY'RE NOT SPECIMENS EITHER!

DID YOU KNOW THAT:

Animals such as dogs, cats, sheep, hamsters, and guinea pigs, and primates like chimpanzees, are used in scientific testing.

About 1.5 million animals are used in research every year, not including mice (if mice were included, the number would be about 10 million!).

Most animals are killed after being used in an experiment.

WHAT CAN YOU DO?

Write to Governor Jefferson and tell him to pass laws to stop testing on animals!

Send letters to: Governor John A. Jefferson
State Capitol
Albany, NY 11111

Sketch out your rough draft here:

See the box on page 220 for some ideas

↓

ATTENTION-GRABBING HEADLINE OR SLOGAN:

CHECK OUT
DOSOMETHING.ORG/BOOK
FOR MORE: *Fact Sheet*
templates

SOURCE OF THE PHOTO OR PICTURE YOU WANT TO USE:

FACT #1

FACT #2

FACT #3

FACT #4

WHAT CAN PEOPLE DO?

✳ *Real stories are powerful! See if you can get a quote from an expert or someone who has been personally affected by your Thing.*

KNOW YOUR AUDIENCE. Who do you want to see this? Other kids? Grown-ups? Make sure your language and style will draw in the people you're trying to reach. Your classmates may like a flyer that uses fun doodles and abbreviations. But the local school board? Probably not.

GET THE RIGHT MATERIALS. What do you need to create these flyers? This may include poster board, access to a computer or copy machine, paint, markers, construction paper, and other fun art supplies.

STAY ORGANIZED. Come up with a clear message that describes what you want your audience to do. Do you want to recruit volunteers? Donations? Do you want people to come to your event? Say it. Don't forget to give people a way to get in touch with you.

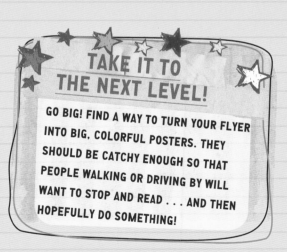

TAKE IT TO THE NEXT LEVEL!

GO BIG! FIND A WAY TO TURN YOUR FLYER INTO BIG, COLORFUL POSTERS. THEY SHOULD BE CATCHY ENOUGH SO THAT PEOPLE WALKING OR DRIVING BY WILL WANT TO STOP AND READ . . . AND THEN HOPEFULLY DO SOMETHING!

Is your thing the environment? How about:

I'M GREENER THAN KERMIT BECAUSE I RECYCLE!

(or)

THE EARTH IS YOURS. SAVE IT!

Do animals have your heart? How about:

WILD ABOUT ANIMALS!

Trying to get kids healthy? How about:

YOU ONLY HAVE ONE BODY. BE GOOD TO IT!

Music education? How about:

DON'T MISS A BEAT!

Want to stop bullying at your school? How about:

IF YOU WANT TO CRY, TELL SOMEONE WHY.

(or)

SEE IT. STOP IT. BEAT IT.

Want to give poverty the boot? How about:

MAKE POVERTY HISTORY.

TAKE IT TO THE NEXT LEVEL!

FEELING REALLY AMBITIOUS? CHECK OUT THESE STICKER AND T-SHIRT IDEAS—THEY'RE ANOTHER GREAT WAY TO DRAW ATTENTION TO YOUR CAUSE.

MAKING STICKERS

So far, your marketing strategy has been all about going big, but small can work, too. Stickers are great for labeling and scrapbooking, but they're also great for spreading your message! And who doesn't love stickers?

1. Put your catchiest slogans on some blank computer labels. Shove them into your printer for quicker results. (The labels should come with printing instructions.)
2. Snazz them up by drawing on them or coloring them in a bit.
3. Post them on your locker, notebook, folders, everywhere! Chances are that people will ask about them, and you'll get another chance to talk about your Thing and why it's so important to you. Or, you could hand them out to spread the news about your event.

MAKING T-SHIRTS

Make a T-shirt with your logo on the front and your slogan on the back. Do it yourself with an old tee and some favorite markers or get one printed professionally at Kinko's or other copy stores. There are also lots of websites that do custom T-shirts. Try www.CafePress.com or www.Zazzle.com.

PROJECT #31: CHAT IT UP

Are you beaming about the clothing drive you're organizing? Feeling totally gushy about writing some e-mails to the troops? If it gets you excited, it could make other people happy—or even inspire them to do good stuff, too. You're doing an awesome thing and people should know about it.

You probably love to text. Or e-mail. Or IM. Maybe you're an emoticon person. But simple LOL doesn't cut it when you're changing the world. Pick up the phone and tell someone what you're doing. That's right—use actual w·o·r·d·s. Talk yourself up!

STUFF: Phone, pen, mouth
TIME: More time than a text. Less time than a game of phone tag.

STEPS:

1. Find the phone numbers of at least three friends or family members. Write them on the card below.

2. Pick up the phone.

3. Dial.

4. Chat! You could give them your Elevator Pitch or just catch them up on what you've been up to.

5. Record their responses provided on the next page.

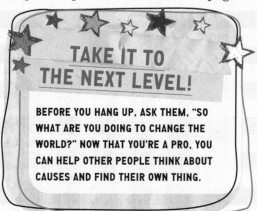

TAKE IT TO THE NEXT LEVEL!

BEFORE YOU HANG UP, ASK THEM, "SO WHAT ARE YOU DOING TO CHANGE THE WORLD?" NOW THAT YOU'RE A PRO, YOU CAN HELP OTHER PEOPLE THINK ABOUT CAUSES AND FIND THEIR OWN THING.

Date: Phone number:
I called:
I told them:

They said:

When I hung up, I felt:

- -

Date: Phone number:
I called:
I told them:

They said:

When I hung up, I felt:

- -

Date: Phone number:
I called:
I told them:

They said:

When I hung up, I felt:

THEY'RE DOING SOMETHING!

NAME: Lizzie Marie Likness, 11, Georgia
THING: Healthy eating

GOOD ENOUGH TO EAT! In an effort
to combat obesity in her community, Lizzie
started baking and selling all-natural goodies
at her local farmer's market, and created a
website to teach people how to cook healthy
food. Check her out at: lizziemariecuisine.com
and DoSomething.org/book.

NAME: Evan Ducker, 14, New York
THING: Discrimination

PROMOTING TOLERANCE Evan was
born with a large birthmark on his face. Evan
decided to educate the public about the medical
and psychological issues facing kids born with
these kinds of birthmarks deal with through his
book, *Buddy Booby's Birthmark*, and his annual
International Buddy Booby's Birthmark Read-
Along for Tolerance and Awareness. Check him
out at: DoSomething.org/book.

PROJECT #32:
PETITION TIME

You've tried to get your principal to get rid of those Styrofoam plates and cups in the cafeteria, and you've given her some good reasons: The stuff is terrible for the environment and it is harmful to wildlife. But your principal still isn't convinced. Frustrating, right? What if you put together a petition and had your entire grade (or school) sign it? Showing that your issue has a lot of support can make a huge statement and might get your principal to change her mind.

"Petition" may sound like a big, fancy word, but it's actually a lot easier to start one than you think. We're going to show you how to do it!

STUFF: Fact Sheet, about 10 sheets of paper (depends on how many signatures you want), clipboard, pens

TIME: A couple of hours to write the petition. About a week to get all the signatures.

STEPS:

1. At the top of the Petition use your Elevator Pitch from Project #11 on page 48. Briefly describe the situation. (You can use the sample on page 226.)

2. Explain what needs to be done, who needs to do it, and be sure to say why it is needed. Keep it short and to the point!

3. Have additional Fact Sheets from Project #11 on hand for anyone who might be interested in learning more.

4. Make a signature page with at least three columns: signature, printed name, date (and if you want, add a grade column).

5. Make sure you have enough signature pages and pens.

6. Pick high-traffic areas to get the signatures. How about the cafeteria during breakfast and lunch?

This is what a petition looks like ↘

WE WANT STYROFOAM CUPS OUT OF OUR LUNCHROOM!

* Styrofoam does not biodegrade easily and it releases chemicals when it gets wet. Those chemicals can contaminate our water supply.

* Researchers found that the chemicals in Styrofoam plates and cups ooze into the foods and drinks we consume. These chemicals get stored in our fatty tissue, where they can build up to levels that can cause all sorts of complications including fatigue, nervousness, difficulty sleeping, and blood abnormalities.

* A lot of recycling plants don't accept Styrofoam because it's expensive to recycle.

★ What is needed: 250 signatures

★ Who needs it: Principal Styro

★ Why it is needed: to get her to consider more eco-friendly options for the lunchroom

SIGNATURE	PRINTED NAME	GRADE	DATE

Use this template to get your petition going!
Cut along dotted line.

CHECK OUT
DOSOMETHING.ORG/BOOK
FOR MORE: *petition*
templates

SIGNATURE	PRINTED NAME	GRADE	DATE

PROJECT #33:
BEFORE THE BIG DAY

The big day is right around the corner. You're excited and maybe a little nervous. You have a team and a location, you've advertised your event, and people have promised to attend or help out. You've done such a good job planning that it would be seriously lame if you forgot something at the last minute. What if you leave your camera at home? What about the Fact Sheets? Or the list of actions people can take after they leave? No worries! Help is on the way!

STEPS:

1. Cut out your "doorman."

2. Decorate him. Give him hair and a mustache. Whatever. Just make it so that you'll notice him every time you turn that doorknob!

> **STUFF:** Markers, pens, and the doorman template on page at right
>
> **TIME:** Does it matter? What matters is that you remember EVERYTHING!

3. Take a look at your Flow Chart from page 203. What can you absolutely, positively not forget? List them on your doorman and don't forget to give yourself a deadline if you need one.

4. On the back, list the things that you'd like to do if possible. For example, it would be great if you could give all the attendees a certificate of recognition or something to thank them for their participation (for a how-to on this, see Project #39 on page 250).

5. Cut out your doorknob sign and hang it on your bedroom door.

Cut along dotted line

STOP!
DON'T
FORGET

TO DO _list_

_____
_____
_____
_____
_____
_____
_____
_____
_____
_____
_____
_____
_____
_____
_____

STOP! DON'T FORGET

WOULD BE NICE TO DO *list*

_____
_____
_____
_____
_____
_____
_____
_____
_____
_____
_____
_____
_____
_____

DOCUMENT IT

CATCH YOURSELF IN ACTION! It's great to have photos and videos that capture all your great work and show other people how much it rocked.

★ **GET YOUR DIGITAL CAMERA,** flip cam, or video camera (if you don't own one, try to borrow one from school, a friend, or a neighbor).

★ **TAKE IT WITH YOU . . .** everywhere! If you're holding meetings, take snapshots of your team in action and videos of your brainstorming sessions.

★ **GET A GOOD MIX** of posed photos (everyone on your team, people you're helping, people who helped you) and candid action shots.

★ **UPLOAD** your pics and videos to a computer or take them to a nearby shop to get them developed if you're using film. (Stay tuned, you'll use these in Project #35 on page 239.)

★ **IF YOU'RE TAKING VIDEO,** think about how you're going to use the footage. Do you want to use it in presentations? If so, you may want a more detailed video. If you're just using the video to remember all the great stuff you did, then you can goof around.

PROJECT #34: THE FLIP SIDE

S o, how's it going? Are you rocking it like you thought you would? Or are things a little bit bumpier than you expected? Sometimes even the best plans don't go the way you thought they would. Maybe getting people to sign your petition is harder than you thought it would be. Maybe you couldn't raise as much money as you wanted. Maybe the local paper decided not to print your letter. Maybe your team is losing energy. Grrr!

Don't beat yourself up if things aren't going exactly as planned. Making a difference can be fun, it can be exciting, but it can sometimes be boring, hard, or frustrating. Feeling bad won't help you get the job done, so it's important to find the good in the bad—it's just a matter of flipping it.

STUFF: A pen and the best attitude you can find

TIME: Enough time to see the silver lining

STEPS:

1. List the negative things you've heard or told yourself about your Thing or your Project on page 233.

2. Now think about how you can change these negatives to a positive.

3. Do this with all the negative statements on your list.

4. Tear out your list and carry it with you— when you hear that little voice of doubt in your head, you can pull it out to remind yourself of the great Thing that you're doing!

← Example →

Negative

1. One person can't really make a difference.

→

2. We're only kids. We have no power.

→

The Flip Side

1. If Martin Luther King Jr. believed this, where would we be?

2. Wrong! We have voices, don't we? If people don't want to listen, we'll just yell louder!

TAKE IT TO THE NEXT LEVEL!

MAKE AN INSPIRATION POSTER. IF YOUR THING IS SOLDIERS, POST IMAGES OF SOLDIERS AND THEIR FAMILIES AROUND YOUR ROOM, IN YOUR LOCKER, ON YOUR BINDER, OR ON YOUR BOOK BAG TO REMIND YOU OF WHY YOU'RE DOING WHAT YOU'RE DOING. ADD A FEW WORDS FOR MOTIVATION: "THEY HAVE FAMILIES, TOO!" OR "THEY'RE FIGHTING FOR US!"

Your Turn

Negative	The Flip Side
1.	1.
2.	2.
3.	3.
4.	4.
5.	5.

233

do it

YOU HAVE ALL THE TOOLS YOU NEED. YOUR TEAM IS READY, **YOU HAVE A GREAT PLAN,** YOU'VE OVERHEARD PEOPLE TALKING IN THE HALLS ABOUT HOW COOL YOUR THING IS GOING TO BE, AND THAT LITTLE PERSON ON YOUR BEDROOM DOORKNOB IS MAKING SURE YOU DON'T FORGET ANYTHING. **IT'S TIME TO TAKE ACTION!** CRACK THIS BOOK OPEN WHENEVER YOU'RE FEELING 'BLAH' TO LOOK AT ALL THE AWESOME STUFF YOU'VE DONE SO FAR. HANG UP YOUR COLLAGES. PUT UP SOME INSPIRING PICS—ANYTHING THAT GETS YOU EXCITED TO ROCK YOUR PLAN! NOW TAKE A DEEP BREATH AND DO IT!

My ACTION PLAN

What I am going to do:

How I am going to do it:

My goal:

Good luck out there!

CHAPTER 5

reflect

it!

YOU DID IT. YUP, YOU TOTALLY ROCKED YOUR THING. WOO-HOO! NOW TAKE A BREATHER, PAT YOURSELF ON THE BACK.

THINK BACK ON WHAT YOU DID. DID YOU DO IT WELL? WHAT WERE YOU REALLY GOOD AT? WHAT WAS NOT SO GREAT? ARE YOU DONE? IS YOUR THING FIXED?

IT MIGHT SEEM WEIRD TO LOOK BACK WHEN WHAT YOU REALLY WANT TO TALK ABOUT IS WHAT'S NEXT. BUT YOU HAVE TO LEARN FROM THE PAST BEFORE TACKLING THE FUTURE. THIS CHAPTER WILL HELP YOU UNDERSTAND AND CELEBRATE ALL THE GOOD STUFF YOU DID SO YOU CAN PLAN FOR YOUR NEXT GIG. IT'S TIME TO **REFLECT IT.**

HOW WELL DID YOU DO?

HOW MUCH DID YOU ROCK IT?

WHO WILL YOU TELL?

HOW WILL YOU THANK YOUR TEAM?

DO PROJECTS #35 — #41 TO FIGURE IT OUT!

HOW CAN YOU PASS IT ON?

PROJECT #35: SCRAPBOOK STAR

Making a scrapbook is a great way to keep track of all the cool stuff you did and helps you remember your awesome experience. Did you take pictures when you rocked your Thing? If you fixed or cleaned something up in your town or school, include before and after shots—like a makeover in a magazine. If you helped other people out, use pics of the actual people. If you started a club, be sure to paste that pic from your first meeting! If you volunteered somewhere for a day, include pictures of yourself and other volunteers hard at work. Be creative and include all the steps of the process. We'll get you started with the blank scrapbook sheet on the next page.

STUFF: Pics, scissors, glue or tape, markers, pens, pencils, photo book, notebook, or poster board, magazines, glitter, stickers

TIME: Depends how crafty you are. Super-crafty? This could take all afternoon. Not so crafty? Two minutes.

STEPS:

1. Sort through your pictures. Which ones show off your work the best?

2. Don't have many pics? Just use what you've got and draw what you don't.

3. Organize your pictures so they take you every step along the way, from Chapter 1, "See It," right on through Chapter 4, "Do It."

4. Cut out words from magazines that explain what you did or how you felt while doing it. Pile on the glitter, the stickers, your own drawings, even add some inside jokes—make it yours.

See It

Believe It

Build It

CHECK OUT
DOSOMETHING.ORG/BOOK
FOR MORE: _blank_
scrapbook pages

Do It

TAKE IT TO THE NEXT LEVEL!

IF YOU FILMED VIDEO, START BY UPLOADING IT TO A COMPUTER. IF YOU HAVE CRAZY COMPUTER SKILLS, MESS AROUND WITH EDITING TOOLS AND CUT A VIDEO. POST YOUR VIDEO ON YOUTUBE.COM, DOSOMETHING.ORG/BOOK, OR ON YOUR OWN WEBSITE TO SHARE IT!

THEY'RE DOING SOMETHING!

NAME: Leonardo DiCaprio
THING: Environment

MOVIE STAR GOES GREEN Leo is Hollywood's green guru, always raising awareness about global warming and climate change, and living green every day. He has filmed his own movie about climate change and started his own foundation to raise awareness about the issue. He also worked alongside the Natural Resources Defense Council, Global Green USA, and National Geographic Kids to make sure everyone knows what they can do to shrink their carbon footprint.

NAME: Sarah Cronk, 16, Iowa
THING: Disabilities

CHEER FOR KIDS! In 2008, Sarah formed one of the country's first cheerleading squads for students with special needs, the Spartan Sparkles. The Sparkles have disabilities ranging from Down syndrome to autism and cheer alongside other cheerleaders at home football and basketball games. Sarah cofounded the Sparkle Effect, an organization that helps cheerleaders across the country start their own squads for people with disabilities. Check her out at: TheSparkleEffect.org and DoSomething.org/book.

PROJECT #36: **IN YOUR SHOES**

In Chapter 2, "Believe It," you had to figure out why you care about your Thing. Now that you've gone out there and done something, have those reasons changed? What did all this work mean to you? Did it make you feel happy, sad, weird, cool, inspired? All of the above? Was it different than you thought it would be? It's good to get these thoughts down before too much time has passed because soon you'll be off on the next Thing. Plus, you'll have your thoughts together when people ask you how your project went.

STUFF: Pen or pencil, your noggin
TIME: Not too long, but give it some thought

STEPS:

1. Fill in the spaces on the card below with your responses.

2. Write three things that you would do differently next time.

I think my project went:

The best part was:

The worst part was:

I wish I had thought of:

But I'm really glad I:

Things I might do differently next time:

1.

2.

3.

PROJECT #37: A FINAL DRAFT

Remember in Project #18 on page 169, when you made a rough draft of your Action Plan? Well, it's not a dream anymore! You went out and took action. You solved your problem. Or at least got a good start.

Go back to that rough draft and see how the real deal stacks up. Time for another collage, using any pictures you took, magazines, newspapers (did you make it into the local or school paper? Cut that out!), and any materials you used along the way.

STEPS:

1. Paste an image on pages 246–247 that represents your Thing.

2. *What* did you do? Find pictures of the "what" and paste them around your Thing.

3. *Who* did you help? If you don't have pics of the actual people, paste in pictures that represent them.

4. *Who* helped you do it? Friends, parents, teachers? Paste their pics or images that remind you of them.

5. *Where* and *when* did it happen? Get pics of these things, too.

6. Break out that rough draft collage from pages 170–171 and compare the two. Did your dream become your reality? Were there things you missed that you want to make sure to cover next time? Write them down on the opposite page.

STUFF: Pictures, magazines, newspapers, scissors, glue/tape, pens, markers, pencils

TIME: Enough time to look back

Write down your thoughts here

The What

I wanted to help: _____

I ended up helping: _____

The Who

I wanted _____ to help me.

_____ ended up helping me.

The How

I wish I had done: _____

I wish I hadn't done: _____

Next time I might: _____

Next time I might not: _____

The What

The Who

The When

The Where

★ ★ ★ ★

★ **TAKE IT TO
THE NEXT LEVEL!**

COMBINE YOUR TWO COLLAGES AND
DRAW ARROWS TO SHOW HOW YOUR
DREAM BECAME A REALITY. WERE YOU
GOING TO MAKE YOUR SCHOOL MORE
ECO-FRIENDLY BUT ENDED UP
GREENING YOUR LOCAL REC CENTER
INSTEAD? DRAW A BIG FAT ARROW
FROM A PICTURE OF A SCHOOL TO A
PIC OF THAT REC CENTER.

PROJECT #38: NUMBERS GAME PART 2

Y ou started out with some firm goals. (Remember that Fix-it Number from Project #14 on page 64?) Did you meet that goal? Did your goal change along the way? When you know how much you did, you can brag about it to people. You can also see how much there's left to do (if any). Go back to your original Problem Number and Fix-it Number and calculate the difference.

STEPS:

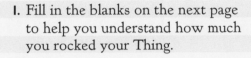

> **STUFF:** Pens or markers
>
> **TIME:** Less time than it took you the first time around

1. Fill in the blanks on the next page to help you understand how much you rocked your Thing.

2. Look at your original Problem Number. Did it change? Why?

3. Look at your original Fix-it Number. Did you meet your original goal? Did you do more? Less? Why?

My Problem Number was _____.

Once I started my project, my Problem

Number changed to _____

because I figured out that _____

_____.

My Fix-it Number was _____.

In the end my Fix-it Number changed to

_____ because _____

_____.

FIX-IT-NUMBER EXAMPLES

★ I helped 15 animals find homes.

★ I collected 500 recyclable cans.

★ I raised $200 for diabetes research.

★ I donated 800 cans of food to a food bank.

★ I spent three hours cleaning the local park.

★ I collected six bags of trash from a local playground.

★ I got 60 signatures on my petition to stop whaling in Japan.

PROJECT #39: THANK YOU TIME

Your project was your idea, so pat yourself on the back. But you probably couldn't have done it without the help of a lot of people. Your artist friend made those posters look amazing. Your writer friend penned a great article for the local paper. Your art teacher donated poster board and art supplies. You need to thank all of those people for their support and acknowledge their hard work. E-mails are okay, but there's nothing like a handwritten note. People remember notes, because who uses snail mail anymore?! Your note will stand out.

> **STUFF:** Nice stationery or cards, envelopes, stamps
>
> **TIME:** Depends on how many people you need to thank

STEPS:

1. Make a list of everyone who helped you and deserves some thanks.

2. Get the mailing addresses for anyone ✳ you'd like to send a thank-you note to. Hopefully you've been collecting their contact info along the way.

3. Get writing! Make it fun, invite some friends over, pump up the music, lay out the snacks, and get those notes written quickly! You can use the template opposite or write your own—just make sure that the note sounds like you.

✳ If you volunteered somewhere for the day, thank the people who showed you the ropes once you got there. If people donated food, money, or other kinds of help, thank them for that. If you are part of a club, organization, or project, include the name of the group at the beginning of the note.

General Thank-You Letter

[name of helper]

[address of helper]

Dear [name]:

On behalf of [name of organization/club/project] I want to thank you for [what did they do?]. Your commitment to helping [your project] is really appreciated.

I was trying to solve the problem of [your Thing] in our [town/school/state/country/world], and your kindness helped me achieve my goal of [your goal]. I was able to [details about what you did].

Throw in some numbers and description. People love to hear about how they helped you reach your goal.

My goal is to continue to make a difference in the [your Thing]. With your continued help, I hope to [upcoming projects or goals] in the next [estimated time for future projects].

Thanks again for your generous support of my efforts.

Best wishes,

[your signature]

Sign here and print your name below. If you have a title, add it below your name.

Volunteer Thank-You Letter

> You couldn't have done it without volunteers. Be sure to let them know you appreciate their help.

Dear [name of volunteer]:

On behalf of [name of organization/club/project] I want to thank you for generously giving your time and volunteering on [date].

I was trying to solve the problem of [your Thing] in our [town/school/state/country/world], and your volunteer hours helped us get closer to [your goal].

I hope you had a good experience, too, and if you'd like to volunteer at upcoming events and fund-raisers, please let me know.

Next up I hope to [upcoming projects or goals].

Thanks again for volunteering. Your support is really appreciated.

Best wishes,

[your signature]

CHECK OUT
DOSOMETHING.ORG/BOOK
FOR MORE: _blank certificates_

TAKE IT TO THE NEXT LEVEL!

HOW ABOUT CREATING A CERTIFICATE OF RECOGNITION? IT'S A GREAT WAY TO SHOW YOUR TEAM MEMBERS THAT YOU APPRECIATE HOW HARD THEY WORKED. AND THEY'LL HAVE SOMETHING TO REMIND THEM OF THE IMPORTANT THING THEY DID! USE THE ONE ON THE RIGHT OR MAKE YOUR OWN.

Certificate of Recognition

Presented to

_____

Awarded this certificate by _____

in appreciation for _____

on _____

PROJECT #40: LETTER TO THE EDITOR

I t is important to share what you did with as many people as possible, if only to inspire other people and get the credit you deserve! Send an e-mail or letter to the editor of your local paper and tell them what you accomplished. Maybe they'll publish it. You never know—your letter might inspire a couch potato to get up and join you in rocking your Thing (or their own!).

STEPS:

> **STUFF:**
> Computer and printer, or pen and paper, envelopes and stamps
>
> **TIME:** You want to get it right. About an hour.

1. Write your letter based on the template on the next page *or* switch it up and write your own letter. If you have access to a computer, you should type your letter. Some tips:

   - *Write clearly. Short sentences get your point across better.*
   - *Double-space your letter.*
   - *Make sure to proofread. Use spell-check and give it a once-over.*
   - *Sign and print your full name and include your address and phone number (the paper might want to get in touch with you to verify some things).*
   - *Put the most important info at the top – sometimes they don't read the whole thing, so get to the good stuff first.*

2. Send it to your local paper. You can usually find their address on the inside of the first page on something called a "masthead."

To the Editor:

Did you know that _____ is a big
[YOUR THING]

problem in _____? That is why I and
[CITY/TOWN/STATE/COUNTRY/WORLD]

_____ are working to
[NAME OF GROUP OR ORGANIZATION]

_____
[INCLUDE YOUR GOAL HERE]

What we hope to accomplish is _____
[TWO SENTENCES ABOUT YOUR PROJECT]

_____
[FACTS TO MAKE YOUR POINT]

_____.

If more people in _____
[CITY/TOWN/STATE/COUNTRY/WORLD]

got involved in this project or one like it, we could do even more

to help _____.
[THE PROBLEM YOU'RE TRYING TO SOLVE]

Sincerely yours,

_____

[YOUR NAME]

[YOUR ADDRESS AND PHONE NUMBER]

PROJECT #41: PASS IT ON

Did you volunteer and can't wait to go back for more? Are you looking to grow your project, maybe even get more peeps on board? Stop reading here! You did something and you want to keep rocking it. Reflect It—jump to the Recap on pages 260–262.

But maybe you're sort of over your Thing. Maybe you want to find a new Thing. You could be graduating, switching to a new school, or moving to a new town. Maybe you made the travel team and you don't have any free time. Or maybe you're just not into it anymore. That's cool. If you built something great, there may be someone else itching to take over. Leaving your replacement with a good sense of who they can rely on along with important information and valuable tools and tips is super important. You worked hard to pull all of this together—your replacement shouldn't have to start all over.

> **STUFF:** Your mission statement; poster board; magazines or newspapers; photos from your project, club, or organization; scissors; glue or tape; markers, pens, pencils
>
> **TIME:** More time than it takes to say your mission, less time than it takes to actually do it

STEPS:

1. Make a folder with all the things your replacement will need to carry on your Thing. Use the checklist on the next page to make sure you have it all nice and neat.

2. Anyone who was super-helpful once might be super-helpful again. (Remember your friend's older sister who drove you to the mall one day? Your replacement should know about her!) List their names and contact info.

3. You've learned a lot. Any words of wisdom you would like to pass on? Anything you wish you knew before you started? Write down at least three things in the space provided on page 259.

Checklist for everything that should go in the folder

☐ **THE NAME OF YOUR GROUP AND LOGO**

☐ **YOUR MISSION STATEMENT**

☐ **A COPY OF YOUR ELEVATOR PITCH**

☐ **ANY FACT SHEETS OR FLYERS**

☐ **A COPY OF YOUR ANSWERS TO IMPORTANT QUESTIONS**
   IN THE BOOK

☐ **IMPORTANT PHONE NUMBERS (LIST THEM HERE):**

   ★

   ★

   ★

   ★

   ★

☐ **LOG-INS TO E-MAIL ACCOUNTS (LIST THEM HERE):**

   ★

   ★

   ★

   ★

   ★

☐ **IMPORTANT PASSWORDS (LIST THEM HERE):**

   ★

   ★

   ★

   ★

Some words of wisdom from me to the person
who's taking on my Thing next!

reflect it

FIRST YOU SAW A PROBLEM. NEXT YOU BELIEVED THAT YOU COULD FIX IT AND MADE A PLAN TO DO SOMETHING ABOUT IT. THEN WHAT?

YOU DID IT: YOU WENT OUT THERE AND ROCKED IT. PHEW! PAT YOURSELF ON THE BACK BIG TIME.

SO WHAT'S NEXT? WANT TO KEEP AT IT? USE THESE PROJECTS TO MAKE YOUR NEXT PLAN BIGGER AND BETTER. OR, GO BACK TO THE BEGINNING AND PICK A NEW THING AND ROCK THAT.

BUT BEFORE YOU GO, TAKE A STEP BACK. GO AHEAD, A BIG GIANT STEP SO YOU CAN APPRECIATE ALL YOUR WORK. YOU WENT FROM NOT KNOWING QUITE WHAT YOU CARED ABOUT TO DOING SOMETHING ABOUT AN IMPORT-ANT ISSUE. AND YOU DIDN'T WAIT UNTIL YOU BECAME A ROCK STAR, THE PRESIDENT, OR EVEN AN OLD PERSON TO DO IT.

SO KEEP AT IT. THIS BOOK WILL BE HERE WHEN YOU NEED IT AND DOSOMETHING.ORG/BOOK ALSO HAS TONS OF RESOURCES. WHATEVER YOUR THING IS, YOU'LL KNOW HOW TO

DO SOMETHING!

I DID SOMETHING!

What I set out to do:

What I actually did:

How much I accomplished:

BOOK IT!

→ →

ORGANIZE THAT GROWING LIST OF THINGS YOU HAVE TO DO IN THIS SUPER-HANDY BOOK IT SECTION. JOT DOWN NOTES, IDEAS, IMPORTANT INFORMATION, AND NOT-SO-IMPORTANT DOODLES. FILL IT IN AS YOU GO—IT'LL HELP YOU KEEP TRACK OF EVERYTHING!

This is your Thing

THING: (Music education)

This should be the number you
came up with in BELIEVE IT

GOAL: Raise [$5,000] for instruments for
your music department

PROJECT/ACTION: Fund-raiser concert for music
program at my school

WHERE: In the auditorium of my school

WHEN: April 15

THE TEAM: Kristin, kristin121@yaboo.com,
555-8955; Travis, tdoz@yaboo.com, 555-4783

Always keep contact info in one spot
so you know where to find it.

CAUSE/THING:

GOAL:

PROJECT/ACTION:

WHERE:

WHEN:

THE TEAM:

PROJECT TIMELINE

Fill in the timeline below with all the dates between now and your project, and keep adding things as you get new deadlines.

Now

✻ If your deadline is months away, you can make an entry for each week. If it's coming up much sooner, you should go day by day.

The Big Day

PEOPLE I NEED

Keep track of who is in charge of what and when they need to get it done.

sample

JOB: Hand out fact flyers at lunch on Tuesday

ASSIGNED TO: Alena

CONTACT INFO: Alena@zaboo.com; 555-1439

JOB:

ASSIGNED TO:

CONTACT INFO:

JOB:

ASSIGNED TO:

CONTACT INFO:

JOB:

ASSIGNED TO:

CONTACT INFO:

PERMISSIONS I NEED

Do you need to reserve a space or get permission to use a space? Need permission to distribute or post flyers? Permission to have a display table at your school, community center, place of worship? Keep track of them here.

—— sample

PERMISSION FOR: Hanging up posters in the library

CONTACT: Mrs. Sullivan

DEADLINE: April 22

PERMISSION FOR:

CONTACT:

DEADLINE:

PERMISSION FOR:

CONTACT:

DEADLINE:

PERMISSION FOR:

CONTACT:

DEADLINE:

269

ALL THE MATERIALS I'LL NEED

- ☐ White paper
- ☐ Colored paper
- ☐ Poster board
- ☐ Markers
- ☐ Pens
- ☐ Buttons
- ☐ Scissors
- ☐ Paint
- ☐ Other (list them here)

EVERYTHING ELSE!

CHECK OUT
DOSOMETHING.ORG/BOOK
FOR MORE: *blank*
pages

Got more to remember? Here are a few blank pages for additional notes.

resources

ANIMAL WELFARE

The American Society for the Prevention of Cruelty to Animals fights for animal rights and safety. They love all creatures great and small—kids, too! Their interactive website is full of pictures, facts, games, and more. Check them out at aspca.org/aspcakids.

The U.S. Fish and Wildlife Service's website has a kids' corner full of fun information and activities that show how the Endangered Species Act helps to protect endangered and threatened wildlife. It highlights a species in "spotlight on a species," tells you how you can help endangered animals, and even links you to a site where you can build a version of your "wild" self. Check them out at fws.gov/endangered/kids.

The People for the Ethical Treatment of Animals have built a website just for kids. Whether you want to boycott dissection at school or take a 30-day vegan pledge, they will give you the tools to learn all about animal welfare. Check them out at petakids.com.

DISASTER RESPONSE & RELIEF

FEMA, The Federal Emergency Management Agency, is the government authority on natural disasters and how to prepare for them. From chemical hazards to wildfires, their website has information on how to prepare for, deal with, and return to normal after a natural disaster occurs. Check them out at fema.gov.

The Home Safety Council is the only national nonprofit that is dedicated to preventing home-related injuries. The website is full of links and resources, and even has a safety guide that includes keeping you, your home, and your kid brother safe. Check them out at homesafetycouncil.org.

The American Red Cross, a historic organization founded in 1881 by Clara Barton, offers care to victims of war and natural disaster. Their website covers disaster preparedness, recovery, and links to local chapters. Check them out at redcross.org.

Architecture for Humanity, a nonprofit design firm, works to create sustainable design for communities around the world, including ones devastated by natural disaster. Their website is full of examples of the work they've completed, and links to their Open Architecture Network, where you can see more real projects and read the stories behind these amazing projects. Check them out at architectureforhumanity.org.

DISCRIMINATION

Southern Poverty Law Center is a nonprofit civil rights organization that fights hate in the United States. Included in their resources are a Hate map, explanations of landmark cases, and their Hatewatch blog. Check them out at splcenter.org.

The Women's Learning Partnership for Rights, Development, and Peace works to end discrimination against women. Their website features profiles on activists, lots of facts and figures, and lists of organizations across the world that work for equality for women. Check them out at learningpartnership.org/resources.

The Federation for American Immigration Reform, a nonprofit, public interest group, is a great source for facts and figures on immigration. Check them out at fairus.org.

EDUCATION

The VH1 Save the Music Foundation works to make sure every kid has access to music

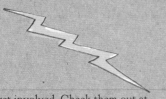

education. Their website is full of easy-to-use information like an advocacy tool kit and an interactive map of schools in the U.S. Check them out at vh1savethemusic.com.

America's Promise Alliance and their 300 national partner organizations work on school dropout prevention. They raise awareness about the approximately 1.2 million students who drop out of high school every year. Check them out at silentepidemic.org.

It's simple: The **National Center for Education Statistics** has the facts. From tables to surveys, this website has all you will ever need to know about education. Check them out at nces.ed.gov.

ENVIRONMENT

The **Environmental Protection Agency**'s interactive website just for kids is loaded with all climate change and global warming info. It's full of links and games about how to help our changing earth. Check them out at epa.gov/climatechange/kids.

Earth911.com dishes out the basics on recycling, green news, and reports. They can even help you find recycling centers in your hometown! Check them out at earth911.com.

The **Natural Resources Defense Council** is a powerful environmental action group, and its website is full of information about green issues. There's a blogroll and featured video clips that all speak to the same mission: safeguarding the earth. Check them out at nrdc.org.

At **Tck Tck Tck**, it's all in the name. Time is running out: the problems of climate change continue to grow. Get the scoop on articles with the latest science and news, explore their interactive climate orb, and read about other ways you can get involved. Check them out at tcktcktck.org.

HUMAN RIGHTS

Amnesty International is the largest human rights organization in the world. They raise awareness about human rights violations across the world, such as petitioning for the immediate release of innocent people who are unfairly jailed. Check them out at amnestyusa.org.

UNICEF—the United Nations Children's Fund—and their website, Voices of Youth, seek to empower kids. Kids can learn facts, read stories, do quizzes, and learn about human rights and development. Check them out at unicef.org/voy.

The organization **Human Rights Watch** investigates human rights violations across the globe. Their extensive research and journalism allows them to cover human rights conditions in 90 countries. Check them out at hrw.org.

The **United Nations** Cyber Schoolbus is a global education tool for kids and teachers. Interactive elements like their database, InfoNation, and a Model UN discussion area, along with quizzes, games, and resources, can teach kids all about the issues that the world faces, from education to hunger. Check them out at cyberschoolbus.un.org.

POVERTY

The **United Nations** has made it a goal for world leaders and their nations to halve the number of people living in extreme poverty by 2015. Their website explains the Millennium Development Goals, and their youth section offers resources and real stories about kids who got involved. Check them out at un.org/millenniumgoals/youth.

Mercy Corps is a team of 3,700 professionals who work to reduce poverty through sustainable community building. Teams help local residents who create positive change in their own communities. They have programs that support 34,000 businesses and increased incomes by 37 percent in 1.4 million households. Check them out at mercycorps.org.

Oxfam's youth website, Cool Planet, teaches kids that there is no excuse for poverty in the 21st century. They explain what they're doing to combat it, like training local health workers and equipping them with vaccinations. Check them out at oxfam.org.uk/coolplanet/kidsweb.

Partners in Health is an organization that provides health and social services to the underprivileged all over the world. An online model on their site shows you how their org really works, and detailed "issues" pages give you a snapshot of the problems they work to solve. Check them out at pih.org.

HOMELESSNESS & HUNGER

The National Coalition for the Homeless is a nonprofit organization that advocates for the homeless and works to prevent homelessness in America. Their fact sheets and publications will teach you things you never thought to ask about homelessness. Check them out at nationalhomeless.org.

The World Food Programme, the largest humanitarian agency fighting hunger in the world, works to help the 1.02 billion undernourished people in the world. They respond to hunger emergencies, help communities rebuild after an emergency strikes, and help prevent hunger in over 70 countries. Check them out at wfp.org/students-and-teachers.

Feeding America, a domestic hunger relief charity, provides food to more than 37 million people in the U.S. Their website highlights a food bank every month, and link you to studies, graphics, quizzes, and fact sheets about hunger in America. Check them out at feedingamerica.org.

HEALTH & FITNESS

The Asthma and Allergy Foundation of America works for advocacy, education, and research about asthma and allergies. Their website will point you to materials, online resources, and publications about the diseases and the people who get them. Check them out at aafa.org.

The Centers for Disease Control and Prevention, part of the Department of Health and Human Services, is a government agency that promotes health and works to prevent disease. Check them out at cdc.gov/gcc/exhibit/kids.

The Juvenile Diabetes Research Foundation International is dedicated to research about type 1 diabetes. Chock full of research, their main website also links to a kids' zone, which provides tips for newly diagnosed kids, breaks down the search for the cure, and has real-life stories and ideas from other kids. Check them out at kids.jdrf.org.

Let's Move is the White House initiative to end childhood obesity. Get resources and information on making healthier eating choices and getting healthier food in your lunchroom. There are interactive games and cool downloadable posters (these could be helpful if you're going to do a poster campaign at school). Check them out at letsmove.gov.

Play60, the National Football League's campaign to end obesity, encourages kids to get active. Watch inspiring videos of pro football players, read tips about healthy living, and just have fun on their interactive website. Check them out at nflrush.com/play60.

VIOLENCE & BULLYING

StopCyberbullying.org is a website dedicated to doing what it says: stopping cyberbullies in their tracks. A trove of useful information can be found within its pages, like Netiquette (that's Internet etiquette), tips on how to recognize and report a cyberbully, and information about the law, for kids of all ages, parents, and educators. Check them out at stopcyberbullying.org.

The **National Crime Prevention Council's** kid-friendly site is devoted to safety. McGruff the Crime Dog offers advice on secrets, crime prevention, and safe shopping. Check them out at mcgruff.org.

The **Brady Center to Prevent Gun Violence** works to keep America safe at home, at school, and at work. Along with facts about guns, victim representation, and their Legal Action project, their website features specific cases—past and present—and the history of the Brady Campaign, and a blog with up-to-the-minute news on gun violence. Check them out at bradycenter.org.

WAR & PEACE

The **Coalition to Stop the Use of Child Soldiers** is fighting for children's rights all over the globe. If you're interested in learning about child soldiers, their website is a great place to start—they have facts, a Q&A section, and links to projects like Red Hand Day (page 162, above) that you can use for action inspiration. Check them out at child-soldiers.org/home.

The **Constitutional Rights Foundation** is dedicated to educating America's youth about law and government and their constitutional rights. In their student section, you'll find myriad topics, tools, and forums, while their main website has facts, publications, and other gems. Check them out at crf-usa.org.

Invisible Children is an amazing group of young filmmakers and activists who make documentaries about children living in East Africa amidst Africa's longest-running war. They use these films to raise awareness and force the international community to work for peace in the region. Their website is filled with resources and information along with inspiring videos and photos. Check them out at invisiblechildren.org.

Save Darfur is a not-for-profit organization working to raise public awareness about the violence and atrocities in Darfur, Sudan. The website will teach you all you need to know about the genocide, its history, who is fighting and why, and what you can do about it. Check them out at savedarfur.org.

GENERAL

From animals to immigration to women's rights, **Change.org** has facts, figures, *and* ways you can take action. Check them out at change.org.

acknowledgements

First and foremost, this book would not have been possible without the ideas and effort of the Do Something team (staff and interns), who always stay at work way past bedtime. Especially: Amanda, Aria, Brittany, George, Jade, Cassidy, Schilit, John, Jordyn, Jessica, Lauren, Megan, Melanie, Fantini, Miles, Nancy, Robin, and all the interns who give us their time, talent, and tenacity. We also want to thank our Board of Directors at DoSomething .org, especially Steve Buffone (and the amazing Jamie Greenberg in his office).

Special thanks to Vanessa and Julia, who gave birth to this book. (Not literally. That would be gross.) But they loved it like two mommies and brought it from little idea to actual reality. Maisie from Workman was another important parent. She made lots and lots (and lots and lots) of great suggestions and changes, and she kept us on schedule!

We want to thank all of our moms and dads. Especially Schilit's.

We have a lot of friends to thank: Quinn from Aéropostale, Phil and Ruby from HP, the whole team at Staples, Clean & Clear, J3, Suzette and Bryan from Colehour Cohen, the EPA, Jennifer and Debby from Sprint, the National Grid Foundation, VH1 and the Save the Music Foundation, Albert and Icema from JetBlue, and the good folks at Channel One.

We need to thank some of the celebrities we've worked with over the last couple of years. You've helped us spread the word! Abigail Breslin, Akon, Ashley Greene, Avril Lavigne, Backstreet Boys, Boys like Girls, Carrie Underwood, Chace Crawford, Ciara, Corbin Bleu, David Archuleta, Dylan and Cole Sprouse, Fall Out Boy, Hilary Duff, Jane Lynch, Joel McHale, Jordin Sparks, Justin Long, Kellan Lutz, Ken Jeong, Kristen Bell, Lauren Conrad, Lil Mama, Mandy Moore, Nick Cannon, Nikki Reed, Peyton Manning, Rachel Bilson, Rihanna, Sean Kingston, the Jonas Brothers, Usher, and the wonderful casts of *90210*, *America's Best Dance Crew*, *Greek*, *The Secret Life of the American Teenager*, and *The Vampire Diaries*.

Julia would especially like to thank: "Vanessa, my partner-in-content, thank you for your encouragement and perspective; John K., for your boundless enthusiasm and tireless effort; Cleary Simpson, for leading me to Do Something; Connie Blunden, for being the first to make me want to change the world; my parents, for your guidance; and my family and friends, for your steadfast support."

Vanessa would especially like to thank: "My little girl Vasialys Solae for being my reason. Julia, we did it! Thank you for being my partner and friend. John Kultgen, you are a joy. Good luck! The Do Something generation for reminding me, inspiring me, and giving me hope. My friends and family for always having my back."

Nancy would especially like to thank: "Jason, Sydney, and Houston for eating so much broccoli, sometimes letting me sleep until 7 a.m., and giving me lots of hugs and kisses."

about the authors

NANCY LUBLIN has led DoSomething.org, the largest online youth-service organization, since 2003. She is the founder of Dress for Success, and has been named to the World Economic Forum's 100 Most Influential Young Leaders. She writes a regular column for *Fast Company* and is a contributor to *The Huffington Post*.

VANESSA MARTIR is the former content editor of DoSomething.org.

JULIA STEERS is the former editor in chief of DoSomething.org.